ALTERED STATES

"OUR NEXT PRESIDENT."—[Drawn by Winslow Homer.]

ALTERED STATES

Alcohol and Other Drugs in America

Patricia M. Tice

THE STRONG MUSEUM

Rochester, New York

Altered States: Alcohol and Other Drugs in America

Published for the Exhibition *Altered States: Alcohol and Other Drugs in America*
The Strong Museum
Rochester, New York 14607
October 24, 1992

Published by the Strong Museum with support from the
Robert Wood Johnson Foundation
Produced for the Strong Museum by Zenda, Inc.
Book and cover design by Patricia Fabricant

Front cover: Exhibition logo design by Kenneth H. Townsend
Back cover: The Court of Dreams, by M. Louise Stowell, 1899, watercolor on paper.
Page 2: "Our Next President," by Winslow Homer for *Harper's Weekly.*
Page 4: An assortment of bottles, jars, and equipment used by Americans in their consumption of drugs.

Copyright © 1992 by The Strong Museum
All rights reserved. No part of this publication may be reproduced, stored in a retrieval system, or transmitted in any form or by any means, electronic, mechanical, photocopying, recording, or otherwise, without the prior permission, in writing, of The Strong Museum.

Unless otherwise stated, all items illustrated are in the collections of The Strong Museum.

Library of Congress Cataloging-in-Publication Data

Tice, Patricia J., 1953–
    Altered states : alcohol and other drugs in America / Patricia M. Tice.
        p.   cm.
    "Published for the exhibition Altered states: alcohol and other drugs in
America, the Strong Museum, Rochester, New York. "T.p. verso
    Includes bibliographical references.
    ISBN 0-940365-05-7
    1. Alcoholism—United States—Exhibitions. 2. Drug abuse—United
States—Exhibitions. I. Margaret Woodbury Strong Museum.
II. Title.
HV5292.T53 1992
362,29'074'74789—dc20   92-35241
                                                                    CIP

ISBN: 0-940-365-05-7

CONTENTS

ACKNOWLEDGMENTS

I would like to thank the Robert Wood Johnson Foundation whose generous contribution has made both the *Altered States* exhibition and catalog possible. I would also like to extend thanks to the board of trustees of the Strong Museum, together with the Museum's President, Dr. G. Rollie Adams, for their enthusiastic support of this project.

Many people have contributed to *Altered States*. Additional support was provided by the B. Thomas Golisano Foundation and WHEC TV 10. David Musto of the Yale School of Medicine and William Rorabaugh of the University of Washington kindly offered their advice and insight. Gordon S. Black and Edgar Adams, Jr. of the Gordon S. Black Corporation and Michael Campo of Rochester Fights Back gave generously of their time and talents, providing encouragement and counsel throughout this undertaking. Michael Harris of the Division of Medical Services, National Museum of American History, gave me access to the rich collection under his care. Other consultants further enriched the project, including Michael Aldrich, Michael Horowitz, Mark Lender, H. Wayne Morgan, and Penny B. Page.

Many members of the Strong Museum staff also deserve thanks, particularly those who worked on the *Altered States* exhibition team, Scott Eberle, Donna Lederman, and Jeannine Lockwood. The Strong Museum Library staff greatly facilitated my research. Kathy Lazar and Carolyn Block persistently located materials and arranged interlibrary loans. Carol Sandler never failed to bring pertinent material from the archives to my attention. James Via, Don Strand, and Melissa Glenney photographed and printed all the illustrations in the Strong collections, an operation carefully orchestrated by Nathan Ruekberg. Conservators Rick Sherin and Elizabeth Morse meticulously prepared artifacts for photography. The registrar's department, particularly Jean Banker, cheerfully and efficiently arranged loans. Monica Simpson and Stephen Feinbloom helped track down various inquiries and each provided a great deal of assistance. Volunteers Esther Elston, Barbara Endter, Alan Mueller, and Alice Ritter located many graphics; their help was no less valuable than their continual patience and good cheer. Lynne Poirier-Wilson, Vice President of Collections and the rest of the curatorial staff assisted me in ways too numerous to mention. Patricia Hogan of Zenda, Inc. edited this publication and offered many helpful suggestions. To these and all other contributors, I extend my grateful thanks.

PATRICIA M. TICE

INTRODUCTION

America has a long history of drug use—sometimes rich and color-ful, other times ugly and tragic. Native Americans smoking tobacco greeted early settlers who brought wine, beer, and "hot waters" to the new world. Colonists considered liquor "a good creature of God" and tobacco the "enchanted herb." Few Americans considered these substances as drugs; liquor and tobacco numbered among the good things in life, necessary to health, essential to trade. By the early nineteenth cen-tury, however, many Americans rightfully worried about the soaring rates of alcohol consumption and the effects excessive drinking wrought upon society. Others cast a skeptical eye on the cultivation of tobacco, which they believed created a thirst for alcohol, exhausted the soil, and bolstered the pernicious institution of slavery.

Nineteenth-century and twentieth-century mainstream America—which is to say the predominantly white middle class—alternated between accepting and rejecting various psychoactive substances. A gen-eration of topers raised a generation of teetotalers, whose own children often saw no reason to abstain until alcohol-related problems climaxed and rekindled the temperance spirit once more.

America's experience with other drugs followed a similar course. Nineteenth-century Americans soothed pain, illness, and anxiety with copious amounts of opium, better known as G.O.M., or "God's own med-icine." Scientific advances in organic chemistry yielded new and more potent drugs such as morphine, cocaine, and heroin. Initially, anyway, these products of modern research appeared to be magic bullets that could vanquish pain and even treat addictions to alcohol and opium. The drugs also offered new routes to pleasure and euphoria, providing an escape from personal anxieties, stressful social and economic conditions, and a relief from the mundane. The poet Omar Khayyam commented on this universal drive for release, "I drink Wine not for Pleasure . . . but to escape a moment from myself."

Enthusiasm for drugs gave way to condemnation as many Americans became addicted to various substances, some unwittingly through medical treatment, others, perhaps more predictably, through recreational use. The result was that by the twentieth century, many Americans began to believe that drugs were inherently bad and that their widespread use unraveled the fabric of society. Mixed up in this attitude were many different threads: a Calvinistic suspicion of pleasure and deep apprehensions about ethnic and racial groups who differed from the majority of Americans in their speech, dress, appearance, customs, and, of course, drug use. All too often, mainstream America's fears about minorities exaggerated and distorted the popular perception of their drug use which, although often not unrelated, became the main scapegoat for disease, unemployment, violence, crime, and cultural decline.

Americans grappled with drug use using moral suasion, medical treatment, legislation, and education. These efforts have sometimes succeeded, sometimes failed, and sometimes been at odds with each other. A predictable pattern of drug use and reaction emerged, a cycle repeating itself over and over, giving credence to the chilling adage that those who do not remember their history are condemned to repeat it.

ALTERED STATES

■ Nicotiana tabacum, *illustrated by this ca. 1795 watercolor, takes its name from Jean Nicot, the French diplomat who introduced tobacco into sixteenth-century France. Like native Americans and some physicians, he believed tobacco could heal ills ranging from the common cold to drunkenness. Many Europeans and Americans inhaled powdered tobacco or snuff, thinking it immunized them from plague. Before long, however, people learned about the addictive nature of nicotine. Elisabeth d'Orleans warned in 1711, "It is certain that he who takes a little will soon take much, and that is why they call it 'the enchanted herb,' for those who take it are so taken by it that they cannot go without it."*

≈ 1 ≈
THE DRUG TRADE
1611–1800

Tobacco and rum fueled colonial America. In a cash-poor economy, each served as currency, and each in its own way helped to shape the American culture.

Tobacco, the source of the addictive drug nicotine, is indigenous to the New World. In the sixteenth century, native Americans, smoking fire sticks of rolled tobacco leaves, introduced the substance to foreign explorers who carried the curiosity to Europe. Demand for the addictive weed grew rapidly, spreading throughout Europe, Africa, and Asia. Many rulers prohibited smoking because they feared widespread tobacco use would drain their national coffers; a few imposed dire penalties on offenders, including the death sentence. King James I of England detested the "stinking weed" and believed that smoking was "dangerous to the lungs." But like other sovereigns, he tolerated tobacco once its great value as a trading commodity became apparent.

Seeking a profitable crop for the struggling Jamestown colony in Virginia, colonist John Rolfe planted a mild variety of tobacco, *nicotiana tabacum,* in 1611. In 1620, as other English settlers established Plymouth Bay Colony in Massachusetts, Virginia shipped forty thousand pounds of tobacco to London. By this time, men and women of all ranks and ages reached for a pipe of tobacco or a pinch of snuff. In 1624, Pope Urban VII strictly forbade church members of either sex to smoke, inhale, or chew the weed, but his words were to no avail. By 1650, an English poet rhymed:

Tobacco engages both sexes all ages,
The poor as well as the wealthy,
From court to the cottage from childhood to
    dotage,
Both those that are sick and the healthy.[1]

Besides being addicted to nicotine, people smoked and chewed tobacco in the seventeenth century because they believed it had medicinal benefits. This view developed from European observations of native Americans who used tobacco in healing and religious rituals. Indians applied tobacco topically to heal rheumatism, wounds, and toothaches, and they smoked it as a diuretic and as a remedy for the common cold. In Europe and the American colonies, people smoked, chewed, and inhaled tobacco, confident that it could expel bodily toxins, neutralize drunkenness, and prevent its user from contracting plague.

As more monarchs and ministers developed a liking for the weed, they no longer saw tobacco mania as an economic threat, but as a financial windfall. Realizing that people would pay considerable sums of money for tobacco, they repealed restrictive laws and levied taxes instead.

Growing tobacco was extremely laborious, however, because the plant required continual tending. The crop did not become truly lucrative until the 1690s, when African slaves took over its arduous cultivation, making the plantation system feasible. Throughout most of the eighteenth century, the South's economy largely depended upon one crop, and that crop was tobacco.

Unfortunately, tobacco quickly exhausted the soil, compelling planters to move ever west in search of more fertile land in Western Virginia, Maryland, Georgia, and, later, in Kentucky and Tennessee. "It is a culture productive of infinite wretchedness," complained Thomas Jefferson, ". . . and the earth is rapidly impoverished."[2]

If tobacco was one object of desire, rum was another. People valued distilled spirits, or "hot waters," because unlike beer and ale, liquor did not spoil. As a more concentrated form of alcohol that consumers could dilute, rum was easier to transport. Like tobacco, rum served as currency. Physicians endorsed the use of distilled spirits (one of the few available anesthetics) believing that liquors such as rum strengthened the heart, prolonged life, warded off fever, nourished the body, and cheered the soul. In the seventeenth century, most individuals agreed with the Puritan minister Increase Mather who pronounced drink "a good Creature of God."

Rum was also a persuasive bargaining tool when trading for land or furs with native Americans. Many settlers and government agents deliberately intoxicated Indians while negotiating treaties, a practice that continued through the nineteenth century. Some native Americans viewed intoxication very differently from whites. Indians believed alcohol connected them to the spirit world, in the same way that mescaline, tobacco, and the self-induced trances used for the same purpose. In this context, later pleas for temperance made little impact. Unfortunately, many native Americans learned aggressive, drunken behavior from whites, and violence within tribal societies consequently increased. As early as 1630, some Indian leaders

■ *After window glass, bottles were the most important and common item produced by glass houses. Glass bottles represented a great advance in food storage, allowing wine and other foodstuffs stored in glass to remain more stable than in other storage vessels. People also used bottles for serving beverages at the dining table, refilling them with wine or rum stored in kegs or jugs. American attempts at glass making initially failed, so throughout the seventeenth and eighteenth centuries, English glass houses supplied colonists with bottles. This English bottle, made between 1690–1710, might have been used for wine or rum.*
Courtesy, Corning Museum of Glass.

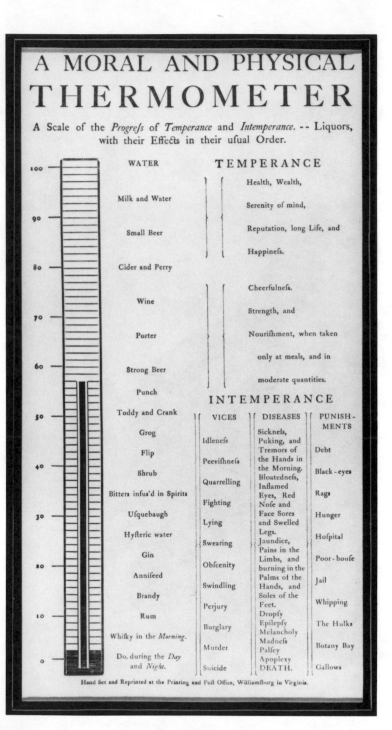

■ *In 1784, Dr. Benjamin Rush issued a warning regarding distilled alcohol in* An Inquiry into the Effects of Spirituous Liquors upon the Human Mind and Body. *Based on medical observations, Rush asserted that immoderate consumption of distilled spirits weakened health, caused various illnesses, and could eventually lead to death. He graphically correlated health, alcohol, and crime in "A Moral and Physical Thermometer," published several years later. Rush's work became a model for later temperance leaders, who by 1850 reprinted more than 170,000 copies of* An Inquiry.

opposed the importation of rum because of its devastating effects on their nations. Settlers, recognizing the link between violence and drinking, were afraid that their own safety might be jeopardized by intoxicated Indians. Although early accounts indicate that many Indians and white men drank together without incident, colonial, and later, state governments issued laws prohibiting liquor sales to native Americas under the pretext that few Indians could drink moderately. The "firewater" myth that stereotypes the drinking habits of native Americans has persisted well into the twentieth century.

In 1657, Boston opened its first distillery to process West Indian molasses into rum. Rum enlivened weddings and funerals, plantings and harvesting, militia gatherings, ordinations, and literally all other private and communal celebrations. People drank a variety of rum-based beverages such as flip, made from beer, sugar, and rum, and grog, hot water and rum. Housewives made possets from curdled milk, rum, sugar, and spices to sooth colds and rheumatism. Edward Augustus, the first medical student to graduate from Harvard, routinely fortified his morning tankard of hard cider with rum, then drank a half a pint of rum mixed with water with his dinner, and warmed the night with a shot of rum as he smoked his pipe.

A dietary staple, rum was an important trade item for Northern colonies just as tobacco was for the colonies in the South. Traders could easily ship rum among the colonies or send it to Canada, Africa, and the non-British West Indies. In the early eighteenth century, New England exported six hundred thousand barrels of rum annually. As the quantity of rum rose, the price of rum fell; as prices fell, social costs rose. Complaints about public drunkenness, poverty, and disorder abounded. In 1686, the president of Harvard College, the Reverend Increase Mather lamented, "It is an unhappy thing that in later years a kind of strong drink called Rum has been common amongst us. . . . They that are poor and wicked too, can for a penny or two make themselves drunk." His son, the Reverend Cotton Mather, echoed similar sentiments when rum prices dipped further in the early eighteenth century. The "Flood of RUM," he observed, "overwhelms all good Order among us."[3]

In reaction to the abundance of cheap liquor and increasing social problems, religious groups advocated a temperate or moderate use of liquor. In 1706, the Society of Friends advised members not to drink distilled beverages in taverns, and later, they prohibited drinking at auctions. By the 1780s, the Methodist clergy, like the Quaker elders, urged followers to shun all distilled liquor.

The distrust of strong liquor was confirmed by the writings of Philadelphia physician, Benjamin Rush. In 1784, Rush wrote an essay, *An Inquiry into the Effects of Spirituous Liquors*, which disputed the traditional belief that distilled spirits prolonged life and prevented illness. Conceding that moderate amounts of fermented beverages such as beer and wine were nutritious, Rush argued that long-term, heavy use of "ardent spirits" destroyed physical and mental health. Rush believed that chronic drunkenness was a progressive disease that the individual could not control once his or her drinking passed beyond a critical stage, and that, ultimately, such chronic drinking could result in death.

The words of Rush, his followers, and concerned clergy went largely unheeded, for about this same time, the whiskey jug replaced the rum bottle in American homes and taverns. The American Revolution lay partly behind whiskey's popularity. Once ties with England and its possessions had been severed, the supply of West Indian molasses declined. As rum supplies dwindled during the war, Americans learned to distill local grains instead. Farmers, who were far removed from urban markets, also found it easier to turn surplus grains into liquid assets. Unlike wheat, whiskey improved with age, did not spoil, and was more easily stored and shipped. Many Irish, Scottish, and Scotch Irish distillers immigrated to America in the late eighteenth century, bringing new technology. Abundant grain, wood, and water supplies made whiskey cheap and plentiful, setting the stage for a significant rise in Americans' consumption of alcoholic beverages.

NOTES

1. A. E. Hamilton, *This Smoking World*, (New York: The Century Company, 1927), 206.

2. H. Wayne Morgan, *Drugs in America: A Social History, 1800–1980,* (Syracuse University Press, 1981), 45. For a good description of the history of tobacco in America, see Jane Webb Smith, *Smoke Signals,* (Richmond, Virginia, 1990), 10–13, and Edward Brecher, *Licit and Illicit Drugs,* (Boston: Little, Brown and Company, 1972), 207–230. Adrienne Koch and William Peden, ed. *The Life and Writings of Thomas Jefferson,* (Toronto: Random House, Inc., 1944), 218.

3. Rum statistics taken from Mark Lender and James Kirby Martin, *Drinking in America,* (New York: Free Press, 1982), 30. Quotes are from Increase Mather, *Woe to Drunkards,* (Cambridge, 1673), 4. Cotton Mather, *Sober Considerations,* (Boston, 1708), 5.

Stills were extremely valuable pieces of equipment made by skilled craftsmen from copper, a scarce and expensive metal. According to historian William Rorabaugh, two hundred dollars would buy either a one-hundred-gallon still or two-hundred acres of land in the early nineteenth century. Thomas Tryon of Philadelphia made this example around 1790, just as Alexander Hamilton, U. S. secretary of the treasury, urged Congress to tax distilled spirits. Hamilton reasoned that the tax would reduce consumption, improve public health, and help fund the federal government. Disgruntled farmers in Western Pennsylvania responded with a short-lived protest, the Whiskey Rebellion. Courtesy, Mercer Museum of the Bucks County Historical Society.

2

"A GOOD CREATURE" VS "DEMON RUM"

1800–1855

Americans steadily drank more and more whiskey during the early nineteenth century as its supply increased and its price tumbled. In the 1820s, when a laborer's average daily wage was about fifty to seventy-five cents, a gallon of whiskey cost twenty-five to thirty cents. By 1830, the annual per capita consumption of distilled spirits alone rose to over five gallons.[1]

Different regions of the country developed distinctive types of whiskey. Pennsylvania and Maryland farmers produced rye whiskey using a mix of corn and rye. Distillers in other areas made whiskey primarily from corn. Bourbon County, Kentucky, distillers created a unique American whiskey—bourbon—aged in charred oak barrels that imparted a golden color and smooth, smoky flavor.

Like rum, whiskey was legal tender. People bartered with whiskey, paid their taxes with whiskey, and on some occasions, paid their ministers' salaries with whiskey. It was also a medicinal and dietary staple because other beverages were problematic. Milk supplies were unreliable; tea and coffee were luxury items. Water—often unpotable—was even more suspect, associated with the spread of diseases such as cholera. Early nineteenth-century handbills advised adding alcohol to drinking water to make it safe. Americans adhered to the traditional belief that alcoholic beverages were healthful, strengthening, and nutritious, an assumption that fostered the practice of drinking to a person's health.

■ *These flasks and the three-gallon stoneware jug hold a total of over five gallons—the American per capita consumption of distilled alcohol in 1830. This figure, however, does not include Americans' consumption of fermented beverages (beer, wine, or cider), nor does it take into account that most women and children drank considerably less than men. Bottles and jugs were in constant demand by distillers and consumers alike. From the 1820s through the 1870s, New England and Midwestern glass houses produced thousands of different pictorial whiskey flasks. Patriotic emblems such as eagles and images of Washington, Franklin, and Lafayette reinforced the idea that drinking was an all-American activity.*

■ *Some drinkers took their drams of liquor in firing glasses. The thick base of a firing glass allowed the drinker to rap it sharply on a tabletop in response to toasts, producing a sound like gunfire. Taverns frequently kept a supply of firing glasses on hand. Members of organizations such as the Masons and Oddfellows often owned their own firing glasses engraved with symbols of their societies or their initials. This English example of nonlead glass was made around 1820. Courtesy, Corning Museum of Glass.*

Liquor varied a monotonous diet: it flavored and tenderized meats and sweetened pastries, while emptins—a leavening agent made from fermented hops—raised cakes and biscuits. Once baked, cooks often soaked cakes with spirits to preserve them or sometimes added liquor-flavored custard. Housewives preserved produce with spirits, packing cucumbers, cherries, and other perishables in brandy or whiskey. This method was cheaper and easier than preparing a sugar syrup or salt brine preservative. They also pickled vegetables in vinegars distilled from wine and cider and sealed jars of potted meats with paper soaked in brandy.[2]

Liquor and socializing were closely entwined, a fact noticed by many observers. In 1842, Abraham Lincoln recalled that whiskey and other intoxicating liquors were

. . . recognized by everybody, used by everybody, and repudiated by nobody. It commonly entered into the first draught of the infant, and the last draught of the dying man. From the sideboard of the parson, down to the ragged pocket of the houseless loafer, it was constantly found. Physicians prescribed it in this, that, and the other disease. Government provided it for its soldiers and sailors; and to have a rolling or raising, a husking or hoe-down, anywhere without it was positively insufferable. [3]

Many Americans celebrated holidays, especially Christmas, the Fourth of July, and New Year's Day, with whiskey, wines, brandies, and punches. But everyday business transactions also began and ended with drams, a small measure of whiskey, about one-eighth of an ounce. Workers commonly stopped at eleven and four o'clock to drink drams supplied by employers who often paid wages partly with cash and partly with daily liquor rations. Irish laborers working on New York's Dwight Canal in 1841, for example, received seventy-five cents a day and three jiggers, or 4 1/2 ounces of whiskey to keep the cold out.[4]

Besides whiskey, people drank a variety of other alcoholic beverages, too. English visitor George Featherstonhaugh stopped at an inn in the 1830s and was delighted to find "Champagne, Madeira, claret, bottled ale, rum, brandy, gin, . . . all the appliances," he rejoiced, "of a jolly existence."[5]

As whiskey consumption accelerated, drinking habits began to change as well. Drunkenness increased so markedly that it caused widespread community complaint and commentary. Some men

■ *"Brandy did the Deed!" exclaimed the title of this ca. 1825 woodcut that depicts a warehouse in flames. Around this time, many newspapers increasingly reported fires, accidents, and deaths caused by an immoderate use of alcohol. The reports provoked reformers to criticize the custom of drinking drams during the work-day. Temperance writer Timothy Shay Arthur observed that the immoderate use of alcohol "wastes our resources" and "crowds the wards of our hospitals." The hazards of on-the-job drinking further increased as many shops and businesses industrialized, substituting powered machine tools for hand tools. Courtesy, American Antiquarian Society.*

■ *Samuel Moore and Company of Southwick, England, made this earthenware wall plaque around the middle of the nineteenth century. In contrast to the delicate pink luster glaze applied to its rim, the plaque bears a grim, transfer-printed image of family violence. Moore and Company took the scene from a series of eight prints entitled "The Bottle," created in 1847 by the English artist, George Cruikshank, whose work was reprinted several times in America. American temperance writer Timothy Shay Arthur also used the prints to illustrate a short story, "The Bottle and the Pledge," published in his book,* Temperance Tales, *in 1848.*

"THE FLOWING BOWL"

Throughout the first half of the nineteenth century, cider (naturally fermented apple juice) was the most commonly consumed beverage in New England and rural areas where apple orchards flourished. Children often drank a diluted version, ciderkins. In 1800, the annual per capita consumption of hard cider was approximately fifteen gallons. Editor Horace Greeley recalled, "Cider was, next to water, the most abundant and the cheapest fluid to be had in New Hampshire, while I lived there, often selling for a dollar per barrel."[1] So essential was the drink that inventors kept the United States Patent Office busy issuing patents for cider mills, presses, and other tools designed to make cider making easier. Like whiskey and rum, cider was legal tender in some states, such as New York, until the Civil War.

By contrast, Americans drank relatively little beer; in 1810 the annual per capita consumption was less than one gallon.[2] The Pilgrims and other settlers had brought beer to the New World two centuries earlier and soon began brewing homemade beers using molasses, ginger, persimmons, spruce, and herbs. Commercial brewing did not thrive. Beer was highly perishable, relatively expensive, and cumbersome to transport. German immigrants, fleeing the revolutions of 1848, introduced lager beer, which became popular after the American Civil War. Lager, brewed from water, hops, and malt, used a yeast that fermented on the bottom of the vat, rather than on the top. Lager (meaning to ripen) was a lighter, less alcoholic brew. Many Germans established breweries still operating today, such as Anheuser-Busch, Schlitz, Schmidts, Pabst, Muller (now Miller), and Schaefer. German newcomers also introduced beer gardens and halls, places where families gathered on Sunday afternoons to socialize and to enjoy music, German food, and lager beer.[3]

Early settlers planted vineyards, but European grapes failed to thrive in the American soil and climate. Native grapes made poor, unstable wines because they were often

■ *Americans stocked their pantries with imported English tablewares throughout the nineteenth century. This ca. 1820 English pitcher, with transfer-printed decoration, is made of creamware, a strong, ivory colored, glazed earthenware. Its inscription invites the beholder to "Come fill your cup and banish grief," promising that "Joy from Drinking shall arise," a common sentiment in both England and America at the time. Pitchers like this one might have been used to serve toddies— whiskey, sugar, lemon, and hot water—or other popular alcoholic concoctions known as smashes, slings, and bounces.*

acidic and low in sugar. Wines imported from Madeira, Spain, Portugal, France, and Germany filled the sideboards and wine chests of the wealthy. Although relatively expensive from importation costs and tariffs, wine was an essential feature of upper class parties, particularly gentlemen's suppers. Less affluent Americans made do with homemade wines pressed from local fruits and berries.

Commercial winemaking advanced only after an American planter, John Adlum, experimented with a native hybrid, the Catawba grape, around 1822. Encouraged by Adlum's success, German vintners planted Catawba grapes in the Ohio Valley and on the islands of Lake Erie. Later in the 1840s, Cincinnati lawyer and horticulturist Nicholas

Longworth started his own winery, staffed with German vintners. Within ten years, Ohio was dubbed the Rhineland of America, supplying middle class Americans with the first American champagne-style wine. Despite such progress, wine's popularity among Americans was limited. Throughout the first half of the nineteenth century, the "omnipresent beverage" was whiskey.

NOTES

1. *Illustrated History of American Eating and Dining,* (American Heritage Publishing Company, 1964), 91.

2. William J. Rorabaugh, *The Alcoholic Republic,* (New York: Oxford University Press, 1979), 107.

3. Ibid., 107.

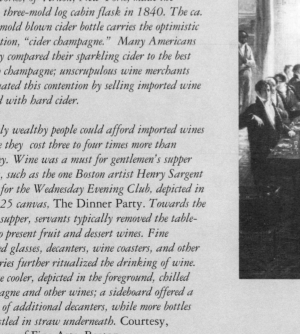

■ *Cider was so deeply associated with the common man that President William Henry Harrison used the image of a log cabin and a jug of hard cider on his winning campaign banner—a neat foil to the aristocratic, champagne-drinking image of his opponent, Martin Van Buren. The Mount Vernon Glassworks, of Vernon, New York, made the blown, three-mold log cabin flask in 1840. The ca. 1850 mold blown cider bottle carries the optimistic inscription, "cider champagne." Many Americans proudly compared their sparkling cider to the best French champagne; unscrupulous wine merchants perpetuated this contention by selling imported wine diluted with hard cider.*

■ *Only wealthy people could afford imported wines because they cost three to four times more than whiskey. Wine was a must for gentlemen's supper parties, such as the one Boston artist Henry Sargent hosted for the Wednesday Evening Club, depicted in his 1825 canvas,* The Dinner Party. *Towards the end of supper, servants typically removed the tablecloth to present fruit and dessert wines. Fine stemmed glasses, decanters, wine coasters, and other accessories further ritualized the drinking of wine. A wine cooler, depicted in the foreground, chilled champagne and other wines; a sideboard offered a supply of additional decanters, while more bottles lay nestled in straw underneath. Courtesy, Museum of Fine Arts, Boston.*

WHO WAS DRINKING?

In the early days of the American republic, drinking was a sign of power and authority, closely connected with politics, business, and military affairs. White males, twelve and over, consumed considerably more alcohol than any other group. Historian William Rorabaugh reported, "It is impossible to obtain an exact accounting, but the American Temperance Society estimated that during each year of the late 1820s nine million women and children drank 12 million gallons of distilled spirits; three million men, 60 million gallons."[1] Female drinking patterns are difficult to track because many women concealed their drinking habits since nineteenth-century mores considered heavy drinking unfeminine and shameful. Many women drank alcohol at social gatherings and in their homes; others abstained totally.

Afraid that alcohol would incite violence or reduce productivity, some states forbade drinking among African Americans—free and slave. Nevertheless, many taverns and groceries sold whiskey to black Americans, and some slave owners used alcohol to reward or control slaves, for example, encouraging them to become drunk on holidays. "All the license allowed," wrote Frederick Douglass, "appears to have no other object than to disgust the slaves with their temporary freedom, and to make them as glad to return to their work, as they were to leave it. By plunging them into exhausting

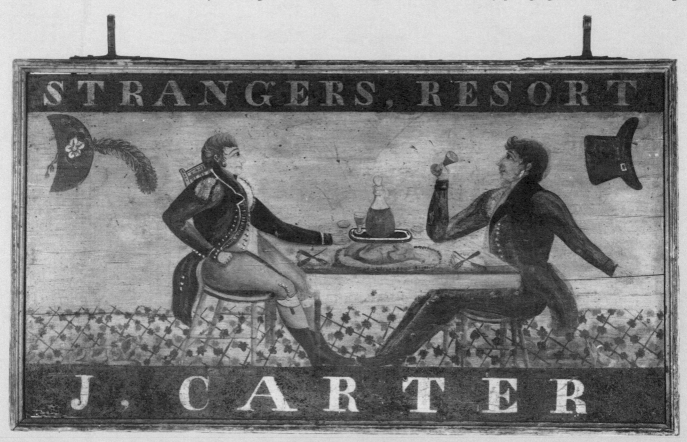

■ An innkeeper named J. Carter hung this early nineteenth-century tavern sign outside his establishment located on the Boston Road (now Route 1) in Clinton, Connecticut. As the sign indicates, taverns frequently served as social clubs where men gathered to drink, dine, and smoke. Taverns offered a convenient meeting spot for political parties and the militia. Trade and professional groups often rented rooms in taverns where they could convene. Other patrons conducted business less formally, sealing a deal with a drink in the taproom. Most respectable women avoided taverns unless necessitated by travel or business; taverns often offered primitive conditions and were frequently the scene of brawling and gambling. Courtesy, Connecticut Historical Society.

■ Since colonial times, political candidates have followed the English custom of treating the voting public to copious amounts of liquor, portrayed here by The County Election, *painted by George Caleb Bingham in 1851–1852. An unstinting supply of liquor bespoke a generous nature; untrustworthy was the candidate who would not drink with the people. George Washington, when seeking a seat in the Virginia House of Burgesses in 1758, provided his supporters with 144 gallons of punch, rum, wine, cider, and beer. "My only fear," he wrote his estate agent, "is that you've spent with too sparing a hand." Courtesy, Saint Louis Art Museum.

depths of drunkenness and dissipation, this effect is almost sure to follow. . . . When a slave is drunk, the slaveholder has no fear that he will plan an insurrection; no fear that he will escape to the North." [2]

Similarly, some towns and counties banned liquor sales to native Americans, although white men broke those laws when doing so was to their own advantage. Some federal agents deliberately intoxicated Indians during treaty negotiations; land speculators frequently conducted business in the back rooms of taverns. In 1832, a federal law prohibited all liquor sales to Indian nations. But whiskey peddlers, called bootleggers because they hid bottles in their boot tops, supplied Indians with whiskey and liquor laced patent medicines.

NOTES

1. William J. Rorabaugh, *The Alcoholic Republic,* (New York: Oxford University Press, 1979), 11.

2. Frederick Douglass, *My Bondage and My Freedom,* (1855; reprint, Salem, N.H.: Ayer Co., 1984), 255.

■ *Taverns were important social centers, as depicted by John Lewis Krimmel's 1813 painting,* Village Tavern. *Taverns fed and sheltered travelers, and in rural areas, functioned as the post office, trading post, stagecoach stop, courtroom, auction house, and gathering place for exchanging the latest news. In Krimmel's painting, a stagecoach halts outside the tavern's door and a man enters, laden with goods, perhaps to trade. This particular innkeeper hung newspapers and an almanac on the walls for the patrons' convenience. His well-stocked bar included assorted punch bowls, tankards, tumblers, and a tin box for sugar and spices.* Courtesy, Toledo Museum of Art.

■ *In the late eighteenth and early nineteenth centuries, many glass houses produced pocket bottles, small flasks that easily slipped into pockets, allowing their owners to carry half-pints or pints of liquor, a day's supply of drams. To make this bottle, the glass blower dipped a gathering of molten glass into a ribbed mold, withdrew it, then twisted it to swirl the ribbing, and, finally, blew the bottle to its present size. Such bottles, common around 1800–1825, are called Pitkin-type after the Manchester, Connecticut, glass house of William and Joseph Pitkin which produced swirled glasswares, although many other American glass houses produced similar work.*

went on solitary sprees, drinking for days or until unconscious. Many cities and towns, such as Rochester, New York, appointed public officials to oversee the welfare of "idiots, bastards, and habitual drunkards."

Public drunkenness was only one aspect of the problem facing early nineteenth-century society. With the rising drinking rate came a multitude of other social ills. As author and reformer Timothy Shay Arthur noted:

It wastes our resources; it saps our national strength; . . . it frustrates our schools; it fills our prisons; it crowds the wards of our hospitals; peoples the cells of our asylums; swells the tables of our mortality; degrades many of our rich, brutalizes multitudes of our poor.[6]

As drinking increased, family violence also became a more visible fact of life, partially because more people lived in towns and cities instead of isolated farms where such abuse was less apparent. Accounts of inebriate mothers neglecting their children spread, but these stories were outnumbered by incidents of wife and child beating. A Penfield, New York, carpenter, Calvin Owen, wrote in his diary,

I have just heard that my cousin Grange Owen is in Rochester Jail for ill treatment of his wife and family. His wife having made legal complaint. He refuses to get bail or give bonds for his future good conduct. I am satisfied that his conduct is bad and insufferable, it is caused in part by his drinking *rum.*

Violence fueled by alcohol knew no social or economic bounds. Aristocratic diarist Mary Chesnut, a keen observer of upper class, Southern life, wrote in 1861: "We all know what a drunken man is. To think, *for no crime,* a person may be condemned to

■ *Sometimes plates and cups manufactured for children's use served up sobering maxims. Like the plaque illustrated on page 23, this plate, made around 1860, by J. and G. Meakin of Staffordshire, England, also bears an image from George Cruikshank's print series, "The Bottle," (1847). The scene depicts a problem common in America and England. Many taverns and saloons allowed patrons to run up sizable bills which led to financial ruin—and worse. Here a penitent wage earner returns to domestic tragedy. His barefoot son huddles by the fire, next to a grieving mother wrapped in old shawls. The father's tattered hat lies on the uncarpeted floor, while in the background rests his dead child's coffin, presumably a victim of malnutrition. Raised wheat decoration on the rim wreathes the scene— as a symbol of bread and abundance, not, conversely, alcohol.*

live with one for thirty years. . . . [E]verybody knows the life of a woman whose husband drinks."[7]

Habitual drunkenness led to lost wages, lost jobs, and lost homes. Typically, the drunkard landed in debtor's prison while his wife and children sought shelter in a county almshouse or poorhouse.

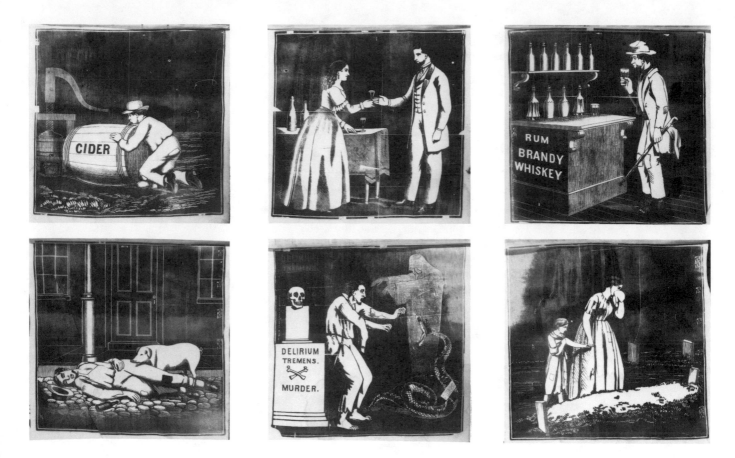

In the eighteenth and nineteenth centuries, artists often depicted alcoholism as the "drunkard's progress." This example, probably made around 1850, consists of six printed cotton banners. Although melodramatic to modern viewers, the banners starkly documented a critical social issue. Alcoholic Luthur Benson recalled in 1879 that he started drinking as a six-year old. His spree drinking led first to poverty and blackouts, and later, unable to pay local fines for drunkenness, to jail. After experiencing wild hallucinations and delirium tremens, he was committed to an insane asylum.

"Intemperance has stalked through our land and devoured our substance," complained one reformer. "And the prison discipline report tells of 50,000 cases of imprisonment for debt annually; in consequence of the use of ardent spirits."[8]

Disease caused by excessive drinking distressed many Americans. Physicians began observing that many illnesses occurred more frequently in heavy drinkers. In addition, chronic binge drinkers manifested withdrawal symptoms called delirium tremens, characterized by muscular spasms, fever, disorientation, and frightening hallucinations, followed by a deep sleep and alcoholic depression or death. Historian William Rorabaugh has suggested that these hallucinations or the "DT's" in which the drinker visualizes himself or herself being persecuted "appear to be rooted in a sense of guilt" that accompanied binge drinking in a Calvinistic society. Alcoholic Luther Benson recorded his own experience with delirium tremens as "the most terrible

■ *Father Theobald Mathew was an Irish priest who came to America in 1849 at the invitation of the American Temperance Union. Mathew led a successful temperance movement in his homeland. In America, he worked with the poor, particularly Irish American Catholics. Many joined his cause and promised "to abstain from all intoxicating liquors and to prevent as much as possible by advice and example intemperance in others." Like most temperance literature, this pledge card displays powerful and contrasting symbolism: the beehive of industry counters the viper snuffing out the flame of life; the tranquil home crowned with abundance opposes the violent house marked by death.*

■ *Many Americans decorated their homes with inexpensive prints, such as this hand colored lithograph, "The Sons of Temperance," published by Kellogg and Comstock, Buffalo, New York, ca. 1850. The Sons of Temperance was a popular organization. Penfield, New York, diarist Calvin Owen recorded that in autumn 1846, "the Order of the Sons of Temperance began to be agitated in the village, . . . and organize we did in Jan. of 1847. The Order of the Sons of Temperance originated in the city of New York in Sept. of 1842, by sixteen men who were much devoted to the cause of total abstinence. . . . From this small beginning, in a few brief years they became very numerous, extending through the United States."*

malady that ever tortured man. The sidewalks were to me one mass of living, howling, and ferocious animals. . . . A human corpse sprang into the doorway . . . and struck me a blow across the face with its icy and fleshless hand from which reptiles fell."[9]

Many citizens grew increasingly alarmed at the growing number of the homeless widows, orphans, and drunkards dependent on public and private charity. Diarist Calvin Owen noted that a local resident, Sam Hunt, "died last night of gravely effection after for years he had been intemperate too. He has been supported by the town for five years." The somewhat inebriated state of the union vexed and troubled many Americans who had once optimistically predicted that a new age of republican virtue would flourish in the land of the free. "Is it not mortifying," former President John Adams chaffed, "that we, Americans, should exceed all other . . . people in the world in this degrading, beastly vice of intemperance?"[10] Something had to be done.

TEMPERANCE

In response to excessive drinking and its attendant woes, a temperance movement swelled in America between 1810 and 1850. The movement had its roots in a similar reform campaign that began earlier in Northern Europe and Great Britain. Religious leaders led the way, sermonizing that drink and vice went hand in hand. Liquor, they contended, separated the drinker from both the righteous and righteousness. They asserted that chronic alcohol use destroyed health, ultimately making the drunkard a burden on his or her family and society. In 1812, the Presbyterian Church ordered ministers to preach against demon rum. The cry for temperance—moderate alcohol use—swept across the United States with a wave of religious revivals. Secular societies also organized to promote temperance, such as the Massachusetts Society for the Suppression of Intemperance, founded in 1812.

As the temperance movement gained momentum, however, some followers advocated a more stringent view toward drinking. By the mid-1820s, some clergy and temperance leaders reasoned that there was no safe use of alcohol. They believed that moderate drinkers either risked becoming heavy drinkers or that, by example, they risked tempting weaker souls to drink. The most forceful endorsement of this position came from the prominent minister, the Reverend Lyman Beecher. In 1826, he preached "Six Sermons on Intemperance," concluding that the only prudent course was complete and total abstinence—a matter of some controversy even among temperance groups. A Hector, New York, temperance society solved the dilemma by offering members a choice: they could sign a pledge forswearing just distilled beverages (except for medical use), or they could sign a pledge forswearing all liquor. Those choosing the latter received a *T* for total abstinence marked next to their names—they became teetotalers.

People flocked to temperance groups, particularly in the Northeast and mid-Atlantic states during the 1830s and 1840s. The American Temperance Union reported a national membership of one-half million just a few years after its 1833 founding. The Sons of Temperance and the Daughters of Temperance were two other extremely popular societies with local chapters across the

■ *Decorative needlework and samplers—like this one made in 1832 by Elizabeth Mary Silver, aged twelve—spelled out the temperance message too. Young girls made samplers to learn the alphabet, numerals, and the various stitches they would later use as housekeepers. Samplers also recorded embroidery patterns and displayed needlework skills. Girls often made several samplers, each one progressively more complex. Usually a parent or teacher chose the verse. This one warns "the sin of drunkenness," among other things, "distempers the body, corrupts the blood, inflames the liver, weakens the brain, turns men into walking hospitals" and is, in short, "the root of all evil!"*

country. One young lady described her impressions of a temperance meeting she attended in Wilmington, Delaware, in 1842:

■ *This illustration depicts a rousing session of the Washington Temperance Society, or the Washingtonians, as they called themselves in deference to the first U. S. president. They often conducted rallies where speakers delivered stirring and sometimes sensational accounts of their personal experiences with demon rum. Washingtonian John B. Gough was one such member, riveting audiences with his dynamic oratory skills and invoking tears one minute and laughter the next. Although the Washingtonian movement quickly lost its initial momentum, the Washingtonian Home in Boston continued to offer treatment and hope to recovering alcoholics throughout the last half of the nineteenth century. Courtesy, Bettmann Archives.*

We were at a Temperance meeting on Saturday night. . . . Such a speech as was delivered by a Reformed Drunkard, I never heard. He told us of his subjection to King Alcohol for 18 years, of his then signing the pledge also of breaking it. It was perfectly miserable to sit and listen to him. I was disgusted and yet so much amused that I was guilty of being impolite enough to laugh out loud some 5 or 6 times, although I crammed both gloves and handkerchief in my mouth till I was nigh well suffocated.

While temperance societies were well populated by women and young girls, they generally attended meetings to listen rather than to speak.

Diarist Calvin Owen recorded in 1854,

About a week ago a Female named Philkins gave 2 temperance addresses here at the Methodist church. They were written and of the first order of composition, she had a full congregation out to hear her. The Baptist and Presbyterian preachers refused to give or read her notice in their meetings. In Webster she was not permitted to speak from the pulpit and some Rowdies hissed her, but were put down by the sober.[11]

One of the most influential, if short-lived temperance societies was the Washingtonians, a group similar in some ways to today's Alcoholics Anonymous. In Baltimore, a group of six men banded together in 1840 to help one another stay sober. The support and encouragement that they all received enabled them to overcome their dependency on alcohol. Soon others joined the ranks of the Washingtonians, as they called themselves in honor of America's first president, and chapters of Washingtonians sprang up in towns and cities across the United States, enlisting one thousand men within the year. The Washingtonians met regularly and helped one another cope with abstinence. They aided each other in restructuring their lives and helped jobless members find employment. The Washingtonians were a secular group, devoted to reforming the individual alcoholic, rather than to social and political changes. They disagreed with members of the clergy who preached that drunkenness was a sin and that salvation from demon rum came solely as a grace from God. Friction with church ministers ultimately cost the Washingtonians the support of the clergy, and by 1847, the movement declined.

Temperance societies sponsored youth organizations, such as the Band of Hope. Its purpose was to teach children to say no to both alcohol and tobacco—since many believed that smoking led to drinking. New improvements in printing techniques enabled temperance workers to publish pamphlets and books for children and adults. By 1851, the American Tract Society reported the distribution of nearly five million temperance pamphlets.[12]

Simultaneously, a new publishing genre emerged in temperance tales, heart-wrenching novels, plays, poems, and short stories designed to sway the reader to abstinence or temperance at the very least. Among the more notable works was Timothy Shay Arthur's *Ten Nights in a Bar Room*, a play, written in 1854, depicting the reformation of a drunken father whose innocent child dies from injuries caused by a disgruntled bartender. *Ten Nights* was the most widely performed play after *Uncle Tom's Cabin*. Americans attended productions of *Ten Nights* throughout the second half of the nineteenth century.

As a result of the temperance movement, drinking rates sharply dropped from just over five gallons of distilled alcohol per capita in 1830 to slightly less than two gallons in 1840. An English woman traveling throughout the states in the late 1840s commented on the remarkable "water-drinking habits" of the Americans, observing that iced water was available in railroad cars, hotels, waiting rooms, steamers, and stores. Responding to public demand, some innkeepers turned their establishments into temperance houses, alcohol free zones, where guests could "avoid the noise and confusion consequent to the vicinity of a bar room."[13]

Most temperance advocates relied on moral suasion to convince Americans to stop drinking. Others sought legal action to restrict the availability of alcohol. In 1851, Maine enacted the first statewide law prohibiting nonmedicinal alcohol sales. Massachusetts, New Hampshire, Vermont, Rhode Island, Connecticut, New York, Ohio, Michigan, Indiana, Delaware, Illinois, Iowa, and the Minnesota territory gradually followed. Prohibitionary laws were sometimes difficult to enforce, as evidenced by diarist Calvin Owen. In 1854, he reported that a local official's "barn was burnt" by rum sellers because the barn's owner, E. Worthing was "prosecuting *Rumsellers* for violation of Excise Law. . . . [B]urning and destroying property of Temperance men is common among that _____ desperadoes. It's a Rum argument." Most of the dry states eventually overturned prohibitionary laws as drinking and some of the more overt problems associated with it subsided and as the somber question of slavery gripped the nation. Meanwhile, drugs other than tobacco and alcohol were slowly becoming an American way of life.[14]

NOTES

1. William J. Rorabaugh, *The Alcoholic Republic,* (New York: Oxford University Press, 1979), 80, 8.

2. Amelia Simmons, *American Cookery,* (1796; reprint, West Virginia: West Virginia Pulp and Paper Company, 1963), 102.

3. Louis Banks, *The Lincoln Legion,* (New York: Mershon Co., 1903), 60.

4. Richard Stivers, *A Hair of the Dog: Irish Drinking and American Stereotype,* (University Park: The Pennsylvania State Press, 1976), 30.

5. *Illustrated History of American Eating and Dining,* (American Heritage Publishing Company, 1964), 150.

6. Timothy Shay Arthur, *Ten Nights in a Bar Room,* (Chicago: The Goodwill Library Series, 1854), 2.

7. Unpublished diary of Calvin Owen, Penfield, New York, 24 February 1854, Penfield Historical Society, Penfield, New York. C. Vann Woodward, *Mary Chesnut's Civil War,* (New Haven: Yale University Press, 1981), 169.

8. John Marsh, *Putnam and the Wolf,* (Hartford: D. F. Robinson and Company, 1830), 6.

9. Rorabaugh, *Republic,* 169–75. Luther Benson, *Fifteen Years in Hell,* (Indianapolis: Douglas and Clark, 1879), 77.

10. Owen, diary, 19 March 1854. Rorabaugh, *Republic,* 6.

11. For a comprehensive discussion of the temperance movement, see Rorabaugh, *Republic,* 187–222; Mark Lender and James Kirby Martin, *Drinking in America,* (New York: Free Press, 1982), 41–86. Letter to Theodosia Dunham, 12 August, 1842, Dunham papers, Strong Museum Library, Rochester, New York. Owen, diary, 30 January 1854.

12. Rorabaugh, *Republic,* 196.

13. Rorabaugh, *Republic,* 8. Richard Hooker, *Food and Drink in America,* (New York: The Bobbs-Merrill Company, Inc., 1981), 129. *Dewey's Rochester City Directory, 1845–46* (Rochester, New York: Dewey, 1846), 32.

14. Lender, *Drinking,* 42–46. Owen, diary, 21 August 1854.

TEMPERANCE AND HAPPINESS.

INTEMPERANCE AND MISERY.

TEMPERANCE.

SIGNING THE PLEDGE

INTEMPERANCE.

PLEDGE OF THE BAND OF HOPE.

I _____ hereby solemnly promise to abstain from the use of Intoxicating Liquors as a beverage ; I also promise to abstain from the use of Tobacco in all forms, and all Profane Language.   Signed at _____

FROM THE ANTI-TOBACCO TRACT DEPOSITORY, FITCHBURG, MASS.

■ *By the 1830s, churches and temperance societies enlisted the young in the fight against alcohol and tobacco, since many Americans believed that the use of tobacco led to the use of ardent spirits. The Band of Hope was an international youth temperance group that flourished well into the twentieth century. Children wore ribbons and badges designating them as soldiers in the crusade and sang teetotaler songs from temperance songbooks. Youngsters also signed pledge cards, like this example, printed around 1840 by S. Pierson of Fitchburg, Massachusetts, for the Anti-Tobacco Tract Depository.*

"CUPS THAT CHEER BUT NOT INEBRIATE"

In 1820, a cup of coffee was a luxury that few Americans could afford. Temperance minded reformers and writers petitioned Congress to remove the high import tariffs that made coffee four to five times as expensive as whiskey. "The habitual use of coffee," observed *The New Family Receipt Book* in 1819, "would greatly promote sobriety." Bowing to pressure, Congress repealed the tariff in 1830, causing prices to plunge from about thirty cents per pound in 1823 to eight cents per pound in 1830.[1] In 1832, the U. S. army substituted coffee for its daily rum ration, and in the following years, *The Baltimore American* reported that coffee was now "among the necessities of life," and was part of "the daily consumption of almost every family, rich and poor."[2] Some temperance leaders disapproved of caffeinated beverages such as coffee, tea, and chocolate, believing caffeine might incite a thirst for alcohol. Household adviser and author Catherine Beecher, who deleted wine and alcohol from recipes she published, warned that "alcohol and opium, tea and coffee simply stimulate the brain and nervous system. This stimulus is always followed by a reaction of debility."[3] Most temperance leaders took a more liberal view of caffeine; some went so far as to open temperance coffeehouses and to set up free coffee stands next to saloons.

The 1842 opening of the New York Croton aqueduct also helped the temperance cause by providing the public with clean, safe drinking water. Teetotalers such as Senator Henry Clay briefly popularized wineless, "Cold Water" dinners. The Sons of Temperance and other societies erected public ice water fountains and distributed free ice to the poor. Ice water became so popular, particularly with women and temperance advocates, that hotels and restaurants routinely placed it on their tables, a custom still practiced today.

NOTES

1. Francis Thurber, *Coffee from Plantation to Cup*, (New York: American Grocer Publishing Co., 1881), 183–84.

2. William J. Rorabaugh, *The Alcoholic Republic,* (New York: Oxford University Press, 1979), 100.

3. Catherine Beecher, *Physiology and Calisthenics for Schools and Families*, (New York: Harper and Brothers, 1856), 01.

In the 1840s, a number of inns and taverns banished alcohol from their premises to attract the growing number of temperance minded guests and to assure patrons of a peaceful stay. Because these establishments were less likely to be the scene of fighting and gambling, an increasing number of travelers—men and women—often sought out such temperance houses. The development of hotels and the decline of drinking in general gradually reduced the popularity of these businesses.

Admirers gave this water goblet and teapot to Neal Dow, the Quaker mayor of Portland, Maine, who rigorously enforced a statewide prohibitionary law, the Maine Law of 1851. Gorham and Company of Providence, Rhode Island, made the coin silver goblet, presented to Dow on April 14, 1856. Conrad Bard and Son of Philadelphia produced the coin silver teapot between 1850 and 1859. Appropriately, these two pieces were intended for temperance drinks—tea, which, like coffee, became more affordable in the 1830s, and water. For those avoiding the caffeine in coffee and tea, receipt books offered directions for making lemonade, orangeade, root beer, and an increasingly popular beverage—flavored soda water.

A GRAND
EXHIBITION

OF THE EFFECTS PRODUCED BY INHALING

NITROUS OXIDE, EXHILERATING. OR

LAUGHING GAS!

WILL BE GIVEN AT *The Masonic Hall*

Saturday **EVENING,** *15th* **1845.**

30 **GALLONS OF GAS** will be prepared and administered to all in the audience who desire to inhale it.

MEN will be invited from the audience, to protect those under the influence of the Gas from injuring themselves or others. This course is adopted that no apprehension of danger may be entertained. Probably no one will attempt to fight.

THE EFFECT OF THE GAS is to make those who inhale it, either

LAUGH, SING, DANCE, SPEAK OR FIGHT, &c. &c.

according to the leading trait of their character. They seem to retain consciousness enough not to say or do that which they would have occasion to regret.

N. B. The Gas will be administered only to gentlemen of the first respectability. The object is to make the entertainment in every respect, a genteel affair.

Those who inhale the Gas once, are always anxious to inhale it the second time. There is not an exception to this rule.

No language can describe the delightful sensation produced. Robert Southey, (poet) once said that " the atmosphere of the highest of all possible heavens must be composed of this Gas."

For a full account of the effect produced upon some of the most distinguished men of Europe, see Hooper's Medical Dictionary, under the head of Nitrogen.

The History and properties of the Gas will be explained at the com-

3

"GOD'S OWN MEDICINE"

1820–1900

While alcohol consumption declined in the 1830s, the use of other drugs, especially opium, steadily increased. Opium served as the main pain reliever and panacea for ills ranging from consumption to colic. Although doctors could not cure numerous diseases or perform today's life-saving operations, they could at least ease the pain and discomfort of the sick and dying with opium preparations. "Soft hangs the opiate in the brain," wrote consumptive poet Maria White Lowell before her death in 1853, "and lulling soothes the edge of pain."[1]

Scientists, druggists, and doctors worked to discover and develop more effective drugs to alleviate pain and to combat illness. Morphine, the active agent in opium, was isolated between 1800 and 1810. In 1831, scientists in the United States, Germany, and France simultaneously discovered chloroform, a liquid compound that gives off pain-dulling, sleep-inducing vapors. The anesthetics—ether (a drug made since medieval times by distilling alcohol and sulfuric acid) and nitrous oxide (originally synthesized in the late eighteenth century by English chemist Humphrey Davey)—also came into wider medical use in the 1840s, facilitating new surgical techniques.

Around midcentury, physicians treated nervousness, migraine, and insomnia with products derived from *cannabis sativa,* a member of the hemp family and source of hashish and marijuana. Chloral hydrate, introduced in 1869, later replaced cannabis as the favorite sleeping aid and

■ *"No language can describe the delightful sensations produced,"* exclaimed the fine print of this 1845 broadside announcing a nitrous oxide demonstration. The advertisement reveals Americans' nonchalant attitude concerning certain drugs prevalent in the first half of the nineteenth century. At the time, many people believed that alcohol was the most problematic substance. Like English chemist Sir Humphrey Davey, Connecticut medical student Gardner Quincey Colton believed that nitrous oxide was a preferable alternative to alcohol. Leaving school in 1844, Colton conducted sampling sessions. Twenty-five cents bought an admission ticket and a whiff of the gas. Courtesy, Bettmann Archives.

OPIUM, "GOD'S OWN MEDICINE"

In nineteenth-century America, one of the more widely used drugs was opium, made from the resin derived from the *Papaver somniferum* poppy, native to Turkey and Asia.

Opium had many therapeutic uses. It suppressed coughs and the life-threatening diarrhea that accompanied diseases such as cholera, typhoid, and typhus. Doctors also used opium preparations for childbirth, consumption, arthritis, rheumatism, fever, pain, nervous disorders, and alcoholism.

Its addictive nature was not clearly understood, and like other drugs, no regulations controlled its sale. Druggists,

grocers, general stores, physicians, and later, mail order catalogues, freely dispensed opium preparations such as Dover's Powders, laudanum (tincture of opium), paregoric (decamphorated tincture of opium), and soothing syrups for teething or colicky children. Owing to the scarcity and distrust of physicians, many people doctored themselves with homemade opium preparations by following receipts published in household advice manuals and cookbooks. Just as Cotton Mather once called drink "a good creature of God," nineteenth-century physicians dubbed opium GOM—"God's own medicine."

By the 1840s, when the temperance movement was at

its height, opium imports increased significantly. Physicians observed that their patients became habituated to the drug and were unable to stop taking it. These doctors advised a more cautious use of the drug, but few physicians paid much attention to the warnings. Doctors sometimes mistook withdrawal symptoms for nervousness or other ailments, which yet another dose of opium seemed to cure.

Opium was a balm for strained nerves, as Civil War diarist Mary Chesnut well knew. In 1861, Chesnut became upset when intoxicated guests quarreled at a dinner party. "It excited me so—" she wrote, "I quickly took opium, and *that* I kept up. It enables me to retain every particle of mind or sense or brains I ever have and so quiets my nerves that I can calmly reason and take rational views of things otherwise maddening."[1] Middle class women of the nineteenth century visited doctors more frequently than men—and a great number of women became dependent on medication. Laudanum and other opium based medicines also provided a socially acceptable escape from stress at a time when mores frowned on a woman taking more than the social glass of wine, cider, or punch. "As a rule," wrote one physician, "women take opiates and men alcohol. A woman is very degraded before she will consent to display drunkenness to mankind; whereas, she can obtain equally if not more pleasurable feelings with opiates, and not disgrace herself before the world."[2]

Between 1840 and 1870, opium imports increased seven times faster than the population.[3] Patent medicine companies used large amounts of the drug in nostrums and tonics, prompting addict Luther Benson to utter the following warning: "Shun nothing quicker than the patent medicines which contain liquor, and while you're about it, shun patent medicines which do not contain liquor. The chances are that they contain a deadlier poison called opium."[4]

NOTES

1. C. Vann Woodward, *Mary Chesnut's Civil War,* (New Haven: Yale University Press, 1981), 29.

2. H. Wayne Morgan, *Drugs in America: A Social History, 1800–1980,* (Syracuse: Syracuse University Press, 1981), 40.

3. Ibid., 29.

4. Luther Benson, *Fifteen Years in Hell,* (Indianapolis: Douglas and Clark, 1879), 35.

■ *The United States imported many British patent medicines containing opium, although some American pharmaceutical firms bought opium imported from either London or directly from Constantinople. McMunn's Elixir, for example, was a very popular American product throughout the nineteenth century. Reformer Fitz Hugh Ludlow and many doctors blamed McMunn's for addicting some people who first began taking the product for minor complaints. Overdose was another worry. Numerous accounts record how siblings, left in charge of young children, accidentally administered fatal doses. Diarist Mary Chesnut nearly died twice from doses of opiates ineptly administered in 1865.* Courtesy, Mr. and Mrs. Ralph Schmidt.

■ *This 1887 trade card printed by J. Ottmann, New York, New York, advertised Mrs. Winslow's Soothing Syrup, a popular product for many years, administered to teething, colicky, or "nervous" children. As the image implied, the opium laced syrup quieted the little ones, assuring a good night's sleep for everyone.*

■ *Made for the Great Northern Charity Hospital, this ca. 1890 bottle with its ground glass stopper and pouring lip once contained chloroform, an anesthetic discovered in 1831. Physicians administered the drug to patients during surgery while some individuals, including hashish-eater Fitz Hugh Ludlow, used it for pleasure. Chloroform intoxicated, but unlike alcohol, left no hangover. Chloroform became better known after doctors administered it to Queen Victoria during childbirth. The monarch placed a royal stamp of approval on "blessed chloroform" which she described as "soothing, quieting, and delightful beyond measure."*

sedative among the harried businessmen and middle class women who could afford to patronize druggists. Chloral, wrote Dr. Jansen Mattison in 1879, "has such a wonderful power in bringing sleep and freedom from mental worry and jar." [2]

For the weary and depressed in need of a lift, manufacturers marketed, in the 1880s, a wide variety of cocaine and coca products that promised instant energy and relief from the blues. In 1898, chemist H. Dreser and the Bayer Company of Germany introduced a powerful cough suppressant, heroin. Its potential as a pain reliever soon became apparent, and doctors used heroin—as they did cocaine, morphine, and the other aforementioned drugs—to treat opium and alcohol addiction.

While many new drugs became available in the nineteenth century, it was hypodermic injection that revolutionized how people used them. This technique, which allowed physicians to provide almost instant pain relief by injecting a drug directly into a muscle or the bloodstream, quickly became commonplace in the 1870s. "No one is fully equipped for service in the healing arts without the hypodermic syringe," wrote the *Pacific Medical and Surgical Journal* in 1870.[3] Like the drugs themselves, hypodermic kits were sold over the counter for both medical and lay use. Only after many people developed abscesses and other complications from unsterilized needles or clumsy injections, did doctors and druggists advised that the hypodermic syringe was best left in the hands of a professional.

Drug use also changed for some Americans as urbanization and industrialization accelerated and disrupted folk medicine traditions. As many people moved into cities, they could no longer grow healing herbs and plants. In an increasingly mobile society, Americans often found themselves living far away from older friends and relatives who would have provided advice and help during times of sickness. Into their place stepped the patent medicine industry. Rapidly expanding after the Civil War, proprietary medicine companies personalized and popularized their products by using traditional or grandmotherly figureheads such as Lydia Pinkham of Lydia Pinkam's Tonic. Unlike granny, however, these patented nostrums, tonics, and pills almost always promised a quick fix. Opium, morphine, alcohol, and chloral hydrate were usually the active ingredients. Since manufacturers were not yet required to label a product's ingredients, many people unknowingly developed dependencies to these tonics and elixirs. Customers knew only that they felt well if they took their medicine and that they felt unwell without it.

Some Americans, on the other hand, took drugs solely for their pleasurable effects. A few sea captains experimented with opium smoking in China during the early nineteenth century, but they remained a minority. Then in 1824, English poet and opium addict, Thomas De Quincey, published his *Confessions of an English Opium Eater*. In this colorful and moving account, De Quincey described his addiction to opium. "Happiness might now be bought for a penny, and carried in the waistcoat-pocket; portable ecstasies might be had corked up in a pint-bottle, and peace of mind could be sent down in gallons by the mail coach."[4]

Although initially not widely read, the book later inspired many to try opium. Almost as soon as nitrous oxide, ether, and chloroform were introduced, medical students used them for the same purpose. In 1831, scientist Samuel Guthrie wrote a report on chloroform, commenting that "During

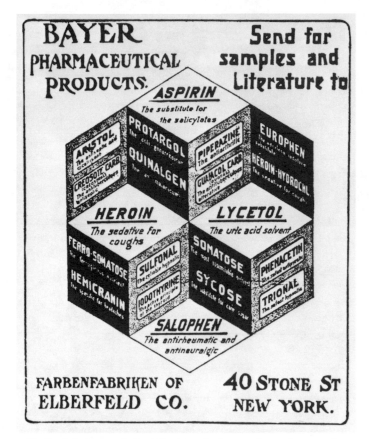

■ *English chemist C. R. Alder Wright first synthesized tetracetyl-morphina, a derivation of morphine, in 1874, but the substance remained little known until the German chemist H. Dreser and the Bayer Company marketed the substance as heroin in 1898. Dr. George Pettey urged his colleagues to use the drug cautiously, in light of the many addicts created by the indiscriminate use of opium and morphine. Nevertheless, many doctors believed heroin was a nonaddictive miracle drug that cured coughs and other illnesses, including alcoholism and cocaine and opiate addiction. Courtesy, Bettmann Archives.*

the last six months, a great number of persons have drunk of this solution . . . to the point of intoxication." University students also threw ether-tippling

MORPHINE, "A RESPECTABLE INTOXICATION"

Morphine, named after Morpheus, the classical god of dreams, is the active agent in opium. Scientists isolated the drug between 1800 and 1810, although most American doctors did not commonly prescribe it until about 1850. They usually administered oral doses of the drug or applied it to an open incision or blister. Hypodermic injection allowed morphine to enter the bloodstream almost instantly, rapidly relieving pain. More potent and predictable than opium, morphine also brought an intense rush of euphoria that led some patients to seek the experience again and again. With the extreme high, however, came an equally extreme low—and, for some, severe withdrawal symptoms. Both the degree of euphoria and of withdrawal differed greatly from the effects of oral opiate use.

Physicians and druggists widely prescribed morphine for diverse medical ills, including sunstroke, asthma, diarrhea, nervousness, and alcoholism. Grocers and druggists sold morphine wrapped in small papers. In March 1865, when diarist Mary Chesnut made a list of groceries needed from the local store, it included "flour, bacon, beef, sausage, . . . morphine and Dover's Powders," a powdered opium preparation.[1]

By the late 1870s, New York newspapers reported that some city residents injected morphine solely for its pleasurable effects. Commenting on the increase in sales of syringes, one account, in 1882, claimed: "People have discovered that they are not only of great service in the alleviation of extreme pain, but that they afford a convenient sort of respectable intoxication."[2]

NOTES

1. C. Vann Woodward, *Mary Chesnut's Civil War,* (New Haven: Yale University Press, 1981), 762.

2. H. Wayne Morgan, *Drugs in America: A Social History, 1800–1980,* (Syracuse, Syracuse University Press, 1981), 27.

■ *Tiemann and Company of New York, New York, equipped this ca. 1860 hypodermic syringe with gold needles. French and English doctors first experimented with hypodermic syringes earlier in the nineteenth century, but the technique was not widespread in America until the 1870s. Like the processing of morphine, hypodermic injection represented a great scientific advance. It allowed a physician to administer a precise and predictable dose of morphine which worked quickly, without nauseating the patient as oral opium doses often did. Those qualities—precision and efficiency—appealed immensely to the nineteenth-century mind which strove to impose order on society.* Courtesy, National Museum of Health and Medicine.

■ *Around 1850, an unknown artist depicted morphine as a beautiful metamorphic poppy maiden who bestowed sleep and oblivion. Morphine was the wonder drug of its time, a more powerful pain reliever than plain opium. A drug isolated and processed by man, morphine represented a triumph of modern organic science over centuries of folklore and trial and error. Some physicians encouraged substituting morphine for the alcoholic's whiskey, arguing that a morphine habit was the lesser of the two evils. Morphine tranquilized while alcohol excited violent passions.* Courtesy, Fitz Hugh Ludlow Memorial Library.

COCAINE, "MAGICAL SUBSTANCE"

Cocaine is an alkaloid obtained from the leaves of *Erythroxylon coca*, a shrub indigenous to South America. European scientists isolated cocaine around 1860 but did not use it widely until the 1880s. Sigmund Freud briefly endorsed its use as a "magical substance" and as a cure-all for opiate addiction, alcoholism, digestive disorders, and tuberculosis. After dosing himself with the drug, Freud observed, "You perceive an increase of self-control and possess more vitality and capacity for work. . . . In other words, you are simply normal, and it is soon hard to believe that you are under the influence of any drug."[1]

In America, manufacturers used cocaine and coca in a variety of medicines including eye drops, toothache drops, and wines and tonics to chase away fatigue and the blues. In 1886, druggist John Strith Pemberston marketed Coca-Cola, an "invigorating" coca drink, although after 1900, cocaine was eliminated from the beverage. The Hay Fever Association also recommended cocaine as its official remedy for hay fever and bronchial ailments.

But by 1885, a few patients became dependent on the drug, manifesting formication, the hallucination of insects or "coke bugs" crawling under the skin. Like morphine and so many drugs before it, cocaine quickly lost its appeal as a miracle drug. By the turn of the century, medical use of cocaine declined because it caused addiction and bizarre behaviors. Recreational use of the drug, however, began to grow.

NOTES

1. Edward Brecher, *Licit and Illicit Drugs*, (Boston: Little, Brown and Company, 1972), 273.

■ *Around 1885, the Cocabacco Company of Saint Louis manufactured Cocarettes, one of the many patented remedies using coca. Piggybacking on the increasing popularity of cigarettes, this company combined Virginia tobacco and Bolivian coca leaves in a rice paper wrapping. The company depicted a woman smoking a cocarette to underscore its point that even "persons in delicate health" could smoke the product. Indeed, the company argued that coca "neutralizes the depressing effects of nicotine" and "gives tone and vigor to the system," making it the "most agreeable and pleasant smoke" for all smokers.*

TEN REASONS WHY
COCARETTES
SHOULD BE USED BY ALL SMOKERS.

1st.—*They are not injurious.*

2d.—*They are the most agreeable and pleasant "Smoke."*

3d.—*They are made of the finest Sun-cured Virginia Tobacco.*

4th.—*They have the exact proportion of genuine Bolivian Coca leaf combined with the finest flavored Tobacco, to produce the most delicious flavor.*

5th.—*The Coca neutralizes the depressing effects of the Nicotine in the tobacco.*

6th.—*Coca is the finest nerve tonic and exhilarator ever discovered.*

7th.—*Coca stimulates the brain to great activity and gives tone and vigor to the entire system.*

8th.—*Coca and Tobacco combined, is the greatest boon ever offered to smokers.*

9th.—*Cocarettes can be freely used by persons in delicate health without injury, and with positively beneficial results.*

10th.—*The Rice Paper used in wrapping Cocarettes is furnished by Messrs. May Brothers, New York, who are the American members of the celebrated French firm that for over 150 years have supplied the trade with this paper, the secret of making which was discovered by their ancestor Henry May. This paper, as now made by the house who conducts its enormous business under the style of "Compagnie Parisienne des Papiers a Cigarettes Francais," burns completely away, leaving no ashes whatever; it dies away in a thin vapor and the smoker inhales only the smoke of the Cocarette.*

IMPORTANT INFORMATION FOR SMOKERS

COCARETTES

TRADE MARK

MAN'F'D BY THE COCABACCO CO.

SAINT LOUIS

COMPTON LITHO. CO. ST. LOUIS.

FAC-SIMILE OF WRAPPER

FOR SALE BY ALL DEALERS

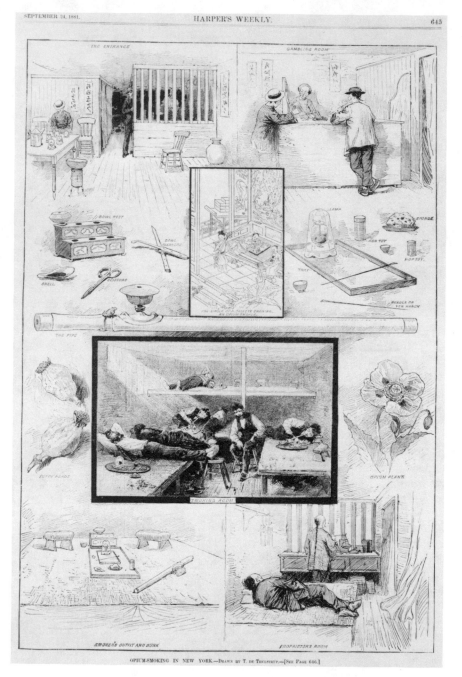

OPIUM-SMOKING IN NEW YORK.—Drawn by T. de Thulstrup.—[See Page 646.]

■ *This illustration published in* Harper's Weekly *(September 24, 1881) depicts the opium dens that flourished in the red light districts of some American cities. Most contemporary accounts describe these dens as dives located behind Chinese laundries; others report more elegant establishments diplaying a lush Turkish decor and catering to both male and female upper class clienteles. The process of cheffing, or cooking opium so that it could be smoked, was long and involved, and the exoticism of the ritual partly added to the drug's appeal. Americans' demand for smoking opium was such that several East Coast "factories" specialized in refining crude opium into a smokable product known as Chinese Heaven.*

frolics and, in December 1844, Hartford, Connecticut, featured a "genteel affair" at which forty gallons of nitrous oxide were administered to all "who desire to inhale it."[5]

During the second half of the nineteenth century, Chinese immigrants introduced opium smoking into the United States. Opium dens thrived in large cities with Chinese populations such as New York and San Francisco. These dens served not only Chinese Americans, but also a small percentage of wealthy men and women, and later, some working class men and women. In a pattern that was to become familiar, recreational drug use often first become a fad of the upper class, later followed by members of the working class.[6] Some individuals found themselves isolated from mainstream society either by extreme wealth or poverty. Unmoved by middle class morality, they often shared a disregard

■ *In 1876, the* Illustrated Police News *published this picture entitled "The Secret Dissipation of New York Belles: Interior of a Hasheesh Hell on Fifth Avenue." During the 1870s, Americans' fascination with exotic Eastern cultures accelerated—and so did the recreational smoking of hashish, a cannabis preparation. Hashish houses, like opium dens, operated in large cities, to the consternation of many who feared an epidemic of drug use. Reformers who thought drugs should be regulated by law stirred up support by presenting images of virtuous young women corrupted by foreigners and their drugs.* Courtesy, Fitz Hugh Ludlow Memorial Library.

■ *During the nineteenth century, druggists and physicians often stocked their supply closets with Tilden's Extract of Cannabis or other cannabis preparations, illustrated by this ca. 1875 glass apothecary bottle. The medicinal use of cannabis increased in the 1870s as more and more Americans found themselves coping with insomnia, headache, and nervousness or neurasthenia as it was then called. The increase of such complaints coincided with accelerating pressures of urban life and industrialization. Cannabis, which relaxed and calmed patients, seemed a promising antidote initially. Some physicians confidently endorsed the drug. Others disliked the drug's unpredictable effects on some patients who experienced unpleasant sensations.*

"NARCOTIC HEMP"

Americans have cultivated *Cannabis sativa* or hemp since colonial times to obtain fiber needed for rope and paper making. By 1840, doctors imported cannabis extracts to treat headache, insomnia, nervous complaints, and hydrophobia among other disorders. Intrigued by reports of its psychoactive powers in Bayard Taylor's popular book, *The Lands of the Saracen* (1855), New Yorker Fitz Hugh Ludlow experimented with Tilden's Extract, a medicine containing cannabis. He later wrote *The Hasheesh Eater,* a work reminiscent of Thomas de Quincey's *Confessions of an English Opium Eater.* "For the humble sum of six cents," Ludlow mused, "one might purchase an excursion ticket over all the earth, ships and dromedaries, tents and hospices were all contained in a Box of Tilden's Extract." He also described the altered sensory perception often produced by cannabis. "The hasheesh-eater knows what it is to be burned by salt fire, to smell colors, to see sounds, and much more frequently, to see feelings."[1] After recovering from his own dependency upon the "narcotic hemp," Ludlow campaigned ardently against the indiscriminate use of opiates, such as McMunn's Elixir of Opium, and for treatment of opium addicts.

In the 1870s, some upper class men and women used hashish, a more potent substance made from the resin and flowering tops of the cannabis plant. People mistakenly believed the drug was a narcotic because it could induce sleep and hallucinations. In 1900, marijuana (made from dried cannabis leaves and tops) was still used in patent medicines and commercial products such as bird seed and paint.

NOTES

1. Fitz Hugh Ludlow, *The Hasheesh Eater*, (New York: Harper and Brothers, 1857), 149.

"ENCHANTED HERB"

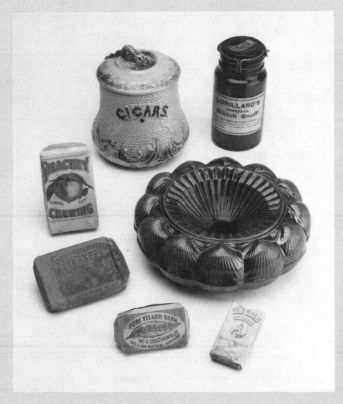

■ *Despite the disapproval of many Americans, the use of highly addictive tobacco products rose throughout the nineteenth century. Manufacturers mass-produced a variety of paraphernalia to support the habit, including pipes, pipe cleaners, pipe racks, tobacco jars and pouches, cigar cutters, kerosene cigar lighters, humidors, smoking chairs, ash trays, cigarette boxes and cases, and rolling papers. Potteries manufactured spittoons, like this ca. 1850 earthenware example, to accommodate the practice of chewing tobacco. Some were plain, some were fancy, some, intended for parlor use, were equipped with ingenious lids.*

"No pleasure can exceed the smoking of the weed"

ADVERTISEMENT, CA. 1875

Tobacco use went through many fads. In the eighteenth century, fashionable men, women, and children inhaled powdered tobacco, or snuff, believing it would protect them from disease. Snuff fell from favor during the nineteenth century, except among the working class and older Americans who clung to the custom. Working class men—and sometimes women too—often chewed "the enchanted herb" because it left their hands free for manual labor. The habit provoked strong protest from many women, including reformer Catherine Beecher who complained about the "puddles of tobacco juice that infest our public conveyances."[1] Many men, and a few women, smoked a pipe. Although women smoked in previous centuries, nineteenth-century society viewed smoking as a manly, and thus, unfeminine habit. Smoking, like drinking, was a male prerogative ritualized at formal dinners when ladies adjourned after dessert, leaving men to smoke cigars and sip brandies.

A Virginia teen-ager, James Albert Bonsack, changed how Americans used tobacco in the 1880s. He developed a machine that rolled 70,000 cigarettes a day, the work of forty hand rollers. Later Bonsack rollers produced 120,000 cigarettes a day. Increased production meant that manufacturers needed more tobacco to process—and more customers. Men, daring women, and young boys increasingly reached for cigarettes, which delivered a standardized dose of nicotine. Because nicotine is addictive, all tobacco products had a built-in market.

NOTES

1. Catherine Beecher, *Physiology and Calisthenics for Schools and Families*, (New York: Harper and Brothers, 1856), 183.

■ *"A Bumper to the Flag" reads the inscription on this pressed lead glass tumbler, made in 1863. The word bumper, an old English term, meant a full glass. Tumbler was also a medieval term for a drinking cup with a rounded or pointed bottom that could not be set down until emptied—lest the vessel tumbled over and spilled the liquid. The tumbler evolved into a straight sided glass with a flat bottom. By 1809, many glass houses including the Bakewell glass house of Pittsburgh advertised tumblers in graduated sizes, ranging from a gill (four ounces) to a quart (thirty-two ounces). By the 1820s, the tumbler had become the standard bar glass.*

authority and an adventuresome spirit that led them to experiment with drugs.

From the Middle East came a strong cannabis product called hashish in the late 1860s and 1870s. Intrigued by Middle Eastern culture, a minority of upper class men and women visited townhouses where they smoked hashish, often in water pipes called hookahs. Hashish candies and confections were also available. Louisa May Alcott, author of *Little Women*, wrote about the craze in a short story published in 1869, "Perilous Play." It presents the tale of several bored young adults who nibbled hashish pastilles on a lark. The drug made one member of the party giggle, another, silent and dreamy. Still, for another young lady and gentleman secretly in love with each other, the drug led to a boating accident, a declaration of true love, and a happy ending in which the young lovers exclaim, "Heaven bless hashish, if its dreams end like this!"[7]

Many reporters and writers were not amused by such antics. In the 1870s and 1880s, the press shocked the public with exposes on the widespread use of opiates and other drugs for both medical and recreational use. Reformer Lufcadio Hearn warned,

The increase in the quantity of opium and its kindred poisons consumed in the United States alone is alarming, and should startle every well meaning citizen. . . . Walk along the streets of this city any day, and you will meet opium-slaves by the score. Its consumption is a disease, and it prevails among mechanical, business and professional men, and is especially prevalent among those of the weaker sex.[8]

Hearn's observation that women of all classes were especially prone to using opiates touched on a sensitive nerve. Women, after all, were charged with child rearing and instilling moral values into the nation's future leaders and citizens. These accounts, and confirmation from the medical community that more and more Americans were indeed dependent on drugs, triggered anxieties about the future of the nation. On top of such concerns was the specter of another old foe. Demon Rum had returned.

THE VINTAGE IN CALIFORNIA—AT WORK AT THE WINE-PRESSES.—DRAWN BY P. FRENZENY.—[SEE PAGE 790.]

■ *On October 5, 1878,* Harper's Weekly *reported on the California wine industry, illustrating "The Vintage in California." By this time, California had emerged as the leading American producer of wines, through the efforts of vintners from France, Germany, Italy, and Switzerland. Hungarian Agoston Haraszthy, the Father of California Viticulture, established the largest American vineyards at Buena Vista in 1870. European immigrants tended the vines, joined by Chinese laborers seeking employment after jobs in the gold fields and railroads declined. Buena Vista produced Zinfandel wine, a white wine that became the trademark of California vineyards, as well as other European-type wines such as Sauvignon Blanc, Pinot Noir, and Riesling. Other prominent California wineries included the San Gabriel Wine Company, which by 1883 included more than fifteen hundred acres, and the wineries of Frenchman Paul Masson and the Italian vintner Second Guarti.*

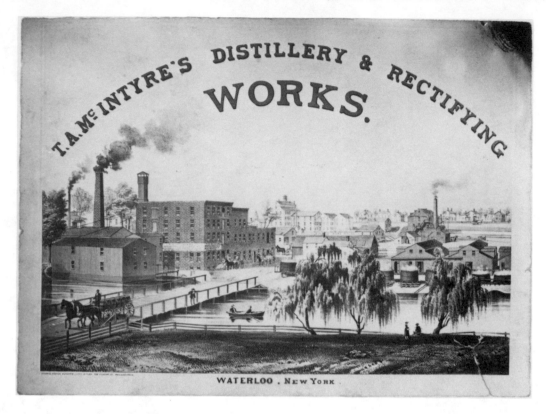

T.A.McINTYRE'S DISTILLERY & RECTIFYING WORKS.

WATERLOO, NEW YORK.

RETURN OF THE CREATURE

During the Civil War, Americans drank more and more, although they never again consumed the record amounts of the 1830s. Alcohol consumption remained fairly constant at just under two gallons per capita throughout the late nineteenth century. America's population expanded greatly in the late nineteenth century, however, providing a large consumer base for alcohol industries.

Commercial wine making initially floundered. The development of native hybrids and the exper-

■ *This trade card advertised T. A. McIntyre's Distillery, Waterloo, New York, in business between 1865 and 1895. As the image indicates, distilling liquor became big business, particularly in the early 1870s. To the nineteenth-century viewer, this trade card was ripe with symbolism of the modern industrial age. The smokestacks belching out black smoke, now offensive to today's ecologically minded citizen, were engines of industry and prosperity. Idle stacks meant unemployment and hard times. The distillery's location near water assured consumers and suppliers access to a relatively fast and efficient transportation network.*

tise of skilled German, Italian, Swiss, and French vintners launched the wine industry in New York, Ohio, and California in the second half of the nineteenth century. Despite progress made by American vineyards, many wealthy and middle class

Americans preferred the quality of imported wines, which also symbolized a cultured taste. *Scientific American* chauvinistically protested: "It probably will be many years before it will cease to be 'fashionable' to give undue credit to wines that are imported, simply because they *are* imported." [9]

Beer consumption rose dramatically after 1860. "Our German friends seem to have imbued the whole American people with their love for *lager,*" reported *Harper's Weekly.* "[W]here, a few years ago, gallons more than satisfied the demand, huge drays laden with kegs are now found insufficient." Americans drank almost 5 1/2 gallons of beer per capita in 1860 and nearly nine gallons in 1870. That figure rose to over eleven gallons in 1880 and almost eighteen in 1890. The increase in beer consumption resulted in part because the Union army issued lager to soldiers during the Civil War, introducing many to the brew for the first time. In the 1870s, improvements in refrigeration, pasteurization, and railroads enabled brewers to produce and distribute larger quantities of lager, which spoiled quickly. Most people carried their own bucket or pail to the neighborhood grocery or taproom because bottled beer was more expensive. Relatively cheap, beer became the drink of the common man.

Distilleries boomed after the Civil War, and the number of licensed liquor dealers mushroomed from 80,637 in 1864 to 204,975 in 1873. Historian Jack S. Blocker, Jr. reports that while the "American population grew at an annual rate of 2.6 percent, retail liquor outlets increased at a rate of 17.1 percent per year." Liquor taxes constituted nearly twenty percent of the federal government's revenues. [11]

■ *"Where a few years ago, gallons more than satisfied the demand, huge drays laden with kegs are now found insufficient,"* reported Harper's Weekly *on the growing popularity of beer and ale over distilled alcohol. Trays such as this one were used in both homes and in saloons. Breweries supplied taprooms selling their brands with bar equipment and also gave them to customers as premiums. This tray advertising Pickwick Ale presented viewers with an interesting mix of images. On one hand, it presented a nostalgic view of the traditional brewer's dray pulled by a team of large horses, but the brewery in the background was unmistakenly a modern, factorylike facility. The German American firm, Haffenreffer and Company, made Pickwick Ale after 1901 for those who preferred an English style beverage.*

Laws required distillers to place their barrels of distilled whiskey into government bonded warehouses for aging. Distillers had to pay tax before they could withdraw their whiskey. By 1885, distillers paid ninety cents or 135 percent on each gallon of

■ *Throughout most of the nineteenth century, people usually carried their own containers, like these stoneware jugs and the flask, to groceries and taverns to buy whiskey drawn from a large keg. But in the late nineteenth century, the production of cheap, throw-away bottles changed the way people bought many foods and beverages, including liquor. Such bottles, like the two pictured here, allowed distilleries to package and seal their products, thus avoiding the adulteration that often occurred when unscrupulous dealers watered down liquor or blended it with other spirits. Customers developed brand loyalty when they could rely on the consistent quality of a particular brand such as O.F.C. rye. A bottle of whiskey was also easier to carry discreetly into a dry state or county.*

whiskey valued at sixty-five cents a gallon before taxation.[12] As taxes raised whiskey prices, some distillers cut expenses by watering down whiskey with raw alcohol, water, tea, cider, and other adulterants, a cause for consumer complaint throughout the late nineteenth century. Less scrupulous distillers and merchants made even larger profits by evading taxes

altogether, selling moonshine or illegal alcohol instead. Moonshiners—those who secretly distilled liquor in mountain or rural hideaways by the light of the moon—matched wits with the revenuers, or government agents, and became the inspiration for many folktales.

Whether made from moonshine or whiskey bottled in bond, mixed drinks or cocktails became popular, and the fame of some hotel bars and restaurants rested partly upon their bartenders' abilities to invent new concoctions. In 1862, New York bartender Jerry Thomas published his *Bartender's Guide,* listing directions for sherry cobblers, flips, smashes, slings, and other cocktails still made today, including versions of the Manhattan and Martini. Many Americans, including Samuel Clemens, alias Mark Twain, believed that a cocktail—or two or three—was good for whatever might ail one. Writing to his wife in 1874, Clemens instructed:

Livy my darling, I want you to be sure to have . . . a bottle of Scotch whiskey, a lemon, some crushed sugar, and a bottle of *Angostura bitters.* Ever since I have been in London I have taken in a wine-glass what is called a cock-tail (made with these ingredients) before breakfast, and before dinner, and just before going to bed. . . . To it I attribute the fact that up to this day my digestion has been wonderful—simply *perfect.*[13]

Hotels and the growth of specialized businesses gradually made the old taverns obsolete by midcentury. In their place came fashionable barrooms and some not so fashionable saloons. Some saloons became notorious for vice and violence. Others served as gathering spots for the working class and political groups. Distillers, seeking reli-

"NOT AS A BEVERAGE"

"Drink no longer water but use a little wine for thy stomach's sake and thine infirmities."

ST. PAUL

Recalling centuries of folk medicine, Americans used alcohol to relieve pain and to treat illnesses. Even the most resolute temperance societies asked members to forswear alcohol only "as a beverage," certainly not as a medicine. During physical and emotional crises, Americans called for distilled spirits, preferably brandy, once known as *aqua vitae,* water of life, because they believed it strengthened the heart and prolonged life. Physicians administered medicines dissolved in wine, which was especially valued for its nutritive properties. If wine was lacking, homemade elderberry, blackberry, and currant cordials substituted. Rye whiskey, mixed with rock sugar syrup, remained a popular cough remedy from the late eighteenth to the early twentieth centuries.

A Northern doctor observed, "those who drink *cyder* . . . can live longer in the cold. . . ." In the South, people believed that mint juleps prevented malaria. To aid digestion, many Americans began their day with a cocktail of bitters, a draught of alcohol infused with bitter herbs, described by one visitor as "a better kind of whiskey a little fortified with spice." Some bitters manufacturers slyly increased the alcohol content of their medicinal products to 44 percent. As the temperance movement grew, many pledge takers shunned whiskey but solaced themselves with bitters instead.[1]

NOTES

1. John Hull Brown, *Early American Beverages* (Rutland, Vt.: Charles E. Tuttle Co., 1966), 92. Richard Hooker, *Food and Drink in America,* (New York: The Bobbs-Merrill Company, Inc., 1981), 280.

■ *With its graduated markings for teaspoons and tablespoons, this ca. 1850 blown wineglass documents the medicinal use of wine. Doctors sometimes prescribed doses of wine, believing it nutritious and invigorating, and they often used wine as a palatable base to which they added healing herbs or powdered drugs such as opium. Though marketed as a health aid, Hostetter's Bitters contained a large amount of alcohol, almost 44 percent. In 1879, author Luther Benson recounted a teen-age drinking spree with his friends: "We were supplied with a bottle of Hostetter's Bitters which was strong enough to make us all reasonably drunk." Hostetter's Bitters was so popular it made its manufacturer a millionaire.*

■ *This ca. 1905 photograph records a typical saloon interior with its mirrored back bar, front bar with the brass foot rail, partition, pictures, and spittoons. The absence of tables allowed more floor space to accommodate customers; table service moreover would necessitate waiters and a larger payroll. Around noon, the saloon keeper may have set up a makeshift table using sawhorses, boards, and a cloth upon which ham, pretzels, and other foods "saltier than the seven seas" were set—free, with the purchase of a five-cent glass of lager. Allegedly the free lunch began in 1871 when Chicago barkeep Joseph Chesterfield Mackin gave away a hot oyster with every drink to lure customers away from competitors.*

able outlets, offered poor but enterprising men bar fixtures and furnishings in exchange for a franchise, making the saloon "the easiest business in the world for a man to break into with small capital."[14]

THE RETURN OF TEMPERANCE

As saloons multiplied, the temperance movement stirred again, this time as part of a broader reform movement aimed at creating a more stable society.

Problems associated with alcohol, such as violence, crime, and disease, continued to plague communities. Americans living in cities became increasingly concerned about accidents on the road and on the job caused by drunkenness. Earlier in the nineteenth century, a wrongdoer might be excused if intoxication caused the misdeed, but in 1881, a judge ruled, "A man who drives carelessly along a highway, and thereby injures a passer-by, cannot excuse his recklessness by showing that he was drunk."[15]

Temperance leaders focused on the saloon as Public Enemy No. 1, not only because saloons led the innocent astray but because they were closely linked with prostitution, brawling, and gambling. Rather than blaming the user, temperance leaders condemned those who plied customers with liquor, free salty lunches, and easy credit.

Liquor led to ruin, injury, and death for many women and children, the most frequent victims of drunken aggression. A woman's wages and property legally belonged to her husband who, if he chose, could spend it on drink, jeopardizing the family home and finances. In the 1870s, some states passed laws that allowed women to sue liquor dealers for damages resulting from the sale of liquor to their husbands or relations. But the burden of redress rested on women once injury had occurred. Few women had the money to pay lawyers; few lawyers wanted civil damage suits because such cases often stalled in court for years.

In December 1873, Hillsboro, Ohio, matron Eliza Jane Thompson led seventy women to local saloons and drugstores where they prayed and sang hymns until the owners agreed not to sell alcohol. Women in thirty-two other states and territories

■ *F. Schmitt, who called himself an "artist photographer," made this photographic carte-de-visite around 1875. His subjects, who apparently chose to stage a card game with drinks as the prerequisite props, posed against a painted studio backdrop. Not everyone thought whiskey was a humorous topic at this time, linked as it was to gambling, corruption, and the Whiskey Ring scandal. A group of internal revenue agents and distillers conspired to defraud the government of liquor taxes by retaining revenues and underreporting the amount of liquor produced. U. S. Secretary of the Treasury B. H. Bristow uncovered the scheme in 1875, seizing distilleries and arresting those involved. The courts convicted 110 persons and recovered $3 million in taxes.*

followed suit in their hometowns. Between 1873 and 1874, fifty-six thousand women crusaded against saloons. Most were white, middle class, native born, and Protestant, between the ages of twenty and forty-nine, who were educated and who had the leisure time for social causes. Many had friends or family members somehow adversely affected by alcohol.

The "praying bands" as they called themselves, drew negative criticism from many, particularly the male working class, and the press inaccu-

■ *Accidental injury and death from drunk driving is not new as this illustration indicates. Newspapers often reported tragedies caused by drunk drivers who lost control of their horses or who overturned wagons, crushing innocent pedestrians. Temperance advocates used this image around 1880 in lectures emphasizing the dangers of immoderate drinking.* Courtesy, Bettmann Archives.

THE BAR OF DESTRUCTION.

■ *Temperance sentiments ran strong once again by the mid-1870s. On March 21, 1874,* Harper's Weekly, *published "The Bar of Destruction." Patrons battle in the back room; a broken bottle, revolver, and old battered hat lay prominently in the foreground. A respectably dressed customer pauses at the bar, as if to choose between rum's death and the future, embodied in his children who beckon at the door. Such imagery was rooted in hard cold fact. Violence among patrons steadily increased in and around saloons, forcing some towns and cities to levy higher taxes on saloon keepers to pay for the extra policing required. More startling and worrisome, chronic drinking and alcoholism, temperance advocates realized, was once again rising among American men.*

rately portrayed them as violent and "unsexed." Some religious leaders condemned these female crusaders as sinners because they spoke in public. Hecklers threw liquor, paint, food, bricks, and stones at the women. In some cities, police blasted them with water from force pumps and arrested them for blocking sidewalks.

Despite these obstacles, the crusaders closed many saloons. Even if the saloons remained closed only for a week or at best for a month, the wives of drunkards and heavy drinkers had time to restock their kitchens or pay their rents. And, as a result of

■ *Between 1873 and 1874, many women took matters into their own hands and formed a Women's Crusade to protest the escalating rates of violence, alcoholism, and poverty caused by increased drinking. Like this group photographed praying in front of a Bucyrus, Ohio, saloon, women conducted prayer meetings outside of establishments that sold liquor, including drug stores which often dispensed whiskey and brandy by the glass. The campaign drew national attention and led to the formation of the Women's Christian Temperance Union.* Courtesy, Ohio Historical Society.

MISS FRANCES E. WILLARD.

■ *At the age of thirty-nine, Frances E. Willard became the second president of the Women's Christian Temperance Union and the temperance queen of America, reigning over the WCTU from 1879 until her death in 1898. Willard used conventional means to achieve radical goals. Praised for her "softspoken and womanly" ways, Willard successfully linked temperance, a topic deemed proper and suitable for a lady's interest, to the broader issues of alcohol legislation and suffrage, prison reform, education, civil rights, and similar areas of social work. Claiming that they were simply protecting their homes, American women followed Willard out of the domestic sphere and into the public arena.*

the crusade, liquor laws, once ignored, were enforced. In 1871, Ohio filed two thousand indictments for liquor law violations; five thousand, in 1874.[16]

In December 1874, a group of women met in Cleveland, Ohio, and organized the Women's Christian Temperance Union (WCTU). Seeing saloons as a threat to their homes, members of the WCTU believed they had a right to close the establishments. "The home is the special care of women," WCTU President Frances Willard proclaimed, "home protection shall be our watchword." Under her leadership, the union became very active. It promoted prohibition and temperance education, demanded a congressional investigation of the liquor trade, and discreetly laid the foundation for suffrage. By 1892, two hundred thousand women had joined. The WCTU gained additional support from another group, the Anti-Saloon League, which formed a national organization in 1895 and fervently campaigned for county laws prohibiting alcohol sales.

Drying up the source of liquor was one thing. Curtailing the drunkard's craving for alcohol was another. Reformers were often dismayed to find that the very individuals they wanted to help seemed totally powerless to help themselves. While the mechanics of addiction were not yet understood, many people recognized that alcohol—and other drugs, particularly opium and morphine—had cast their users into physical and moral slavery. Emancipation, they hoped, lay in medical treatment.

BREAKING THE BONDS: TREATMENT

Around midcentury, a new attitude about drug addiction and its treatment developed as more Americans became dependent on alcohol and other drugs. Although many dismissed alcohol and opium dependency as a willful depravity, some doctors and reformers recognized that chronic dependence on alcohol and drugs required medical care. Temperance supporter, the Reverend Henry Bellows, advocated the medical approach, arguing "Drunkenness is a *disease*, even when it is a moral weakness and a vice."[17]

Treatment for alcoholism was not encouraging. Wealthy and middle class people often consulted privately with doctors who frequently dosed addicted patients with opium, morphine, or other drugs to treat withdrawal symptoms. In many cases, the treatment simply created another chemical dependency. To induce a distaste for alcohol, "a drunkard's medicine . . . was invented some years ago, largely compounded, perhaps, of ipecac or some other nauseating drug," recounted the Reverend Bellows. "But it accomplished no great good."[18]

Household advice manuals, newspapers, and periodicals abounded with receipts for those who sought a discreet and inexpensive cure at home. One such receipt, "by which thousands are said to have been assisted in recovering themselves," called for a mixture of "sulphate of iron, magnesia, and spirits of nutmeg dissolved in peppermint water."[19]

The less fortunate individuals usually wound up in almshouses, hospital wards, and insane asylums. The disorderly found themselves imprisoned in special "DT" or drunk cells. In 1870, 50 to 60 percent of New York City's prison inmates were drunkards.[20]

■ *This ca. 1885 image depicts a drunkard going through alcoholic withdrawal or the "DT's" at the Asylum for Inebriates on Blackwell's Island, New York. Chronic heavy drinkers were often jailed, and some died there for the lack of medical attention. In 1870, more than half of New York City's prison population were allegedly drunkards. Although generally charged with disturbing the peace, loitering, or drunkenness, drunkards often faced more serious crimes, such as robbery, assault, and manslaughter. Because drunkenness was so closely associated with crime, many doctors had difficulty persuading the public that chronic drinking was a disease.* Courtesy, Bettmann Archives.

THE NEW YORK STATE INEBRIATE ASYLUM, AT BINGHAMTON.—Drawn by C. E. H. Bonwill, New York.—[See Page 829.]

■ *An illustration from* Harper's Weekly, *December 25, 1869, presented a congenial view of the New York State Inebriate Asylum in Binghamton. The asylum opened its doors in 1864, although not without difficulty. Some citizens objected to the creation of the institution whose superintendent, Dr. Joseph Turner, emphatically insisted that alcoholism was a disease, rather than a reprehensible moral failing. Turner promoted alcohol research during his tenure. Applicants struggling with alcohol dependencies flooded the asylum. The institution's regime was strict, the cure rate was low, but the asylum offered hope for rehabilitation.*

The lack of specialized care led reformer Benjamin Buller to campaign for a state institution for "alcohol and opium inebriates." The New York State Inebriate Asylum, chartered in 1854, opened its doors in 1864 in Binghamton, New York. Its Gothic style building, located on 252 acres, featured the latest conveniences, including gaslights, steam heat, a garden, conservatory, billiard room, bowling lanes, gymnasium, and a sauna. Since other drugs and tonics failed to cure alcoholism, doctors at the asylum recommended a combination of medicines and months of physical, medical, and psychological therapy to rehabilitate the drunkard or the opium habitué. Progressive as the asylum was, there were locks on all the doors, bars at the windows, and attendants who searched the inmates and their rooms twice a day. Inmates were not permitted to leave the grounds without an attendant. Many middle class and upper class Americans registered there under assumed names to take the cure which boasted a 40 to 50 percent success rate.[21]

Sanatariums opened in the 1870s and 1880s as morphine and cocaine addicts, or habitués, joined the ranks of those dependent on alcohol and opium. Sanatariums generally offered more homelike and personal care than other institutions. In 1870, two doctors, Joseph Parrish and Willard Parker, founded the American Association for the Cure of Inebriates for addiction research and treatment. Dr. Thomas Crothers, a member of the group, opened the Walnut Lodge Hospital in Hartford, Connecticut, for alcohol and opium inebriates in 1880—a facility which parallels some of today's treatment centers for affluent addicts.

Those who were unable or unwilling to undergo medical treatment often tried mail-order cures advertised in magazines and newspapers and discreetly delivered in plain brown paper. The Collins cure and the Woolley cure were just two of many fraudulent products claiming to cure the opium habit. Usually patented cures contained chloral or an opiate base that staved off withdrawal symptoms—for a while. Although they rarely cured, the preparations may have helped some individuals reduce the intensity of their addiction to a more manageable level.

By the 1880s, medical attention focused on opium addiction as more users became addicted and as the particular problems of opium withdrawal became apparent. One addict undergoing withdrawal in 1883 wrote, "I believe hell is composed of opium eaters, and the punishment consists of with-

GEER'S HARTFORD CITY DIRECTORY.   879

"WALNUT LODGE HOSPITAL,"
HARTFORD, CONN.

A Private Asylum for the Special Treatment of ALCOHOL and OPIUM INEBRIATES.

This Institution was founded in 1878 on the modern view that Inebriety is a Disease and Curable. Each case is made the subject of special study and special medical treatment, suited to meet the exact requirements of the case.

This is accomplished by Turkish and Saline Baths, with Electricity, Massage and various other appliances which Art, Science, and experience have proved to be valuable.

Each one is under the direct personal care of the physician and attendant, and experience shows that a large proportion of these cases are restored by the application of exact means and remedies.

Application for admission, terms, and letters of inquiry, should be addressed,

T. D. CROTHERS, M. D.,
No. 142 FAIRFIELD AVENUE, - HARTFORD, CONN.

See page 348 for JOURNAL OF INEBRIETY.

■ *By the 1870s, the wealthy and upper middle class "alcohol and opium inebriates" were able to turn to tasteful private hospitals, such as Walnut Lodge Hospital in Connecticut, which offered individualized treatment. Run by physicians who genuinely believed that alcoholism was a disease, these facilities stressed that inebriety, whether due to alcohol or opiates, stemmed from a physical, rather than moral, deficiency. They developed many theories regarding heredity and cell toxicity to explain the causes of the disease, which helped lessen the burden of guilt carried by many patients. Courtesy, Connecticut Historical Society.*

THE KEELEY CURE

In the late 1870s, former army surgeon Dr. Leslie Keeley marketed his cure for drug addictions, a secret formula called Bichloride of Gold. The preparation was probably a vegetable tonic with gold salts, although Keeley never disclosed the exact composition of his cure, despite charges of chicanery from his rivals. Bichloride of Gold was available through the mail; its cost depended on the type of drug dependency. The tobacco habit required five dollars' worth of tonic per week; alcoholism demanded a nine-dollar dose; opium or cocaine addiction needed a ten-dollar supply.

For the more affluent male and female patients such as doctors, lawyers, and other "intense brain workers," Keeley opened a sanatarium at Dwight, Illinois. Patients came and went at will. Men stayed at the sanatarium, women (who usually came for opiate addiction), rented rooms in nearby boardinghouses and received medical treatment in private. At regular intervals, patients lined up for injections of the gold cure and drank the patented tonic. The staff encouraged patients to take plenty of exercise, to meet with each other to share their experiences, and to support one another. Between September 1, 1892, and September 1, 1893, 14,991 people took the treatment at Dwight.[1] On their return home, patients joined self-help groups comprised of Dwight graduates. The demand for the Keeley treatment was so great that by 1900, there were Keeley Institutes in almost every state.

NOTES

1. H. Wayne Morgan, *Drugs in America: A Social History, 1800–1980*, (Syracuse: Syracuse University Press, 1981), 80.

■ *Dr. Leslie Keeley offered his Bicholoride of Gold cure for chemical dependencies through his mail order business and at treatment centers. At his institutes, patients "passed through the line" four times a day to receive the barber pole, an injection of red, white, and blue medicines. According to historian Wayne Morgan, some assays of the bottled medicine revealed strychnine, atrophia, hyoscine, quinine, and coca. The serum included emetics and apomorphine, which caused nausea if the patient drank alcohol. Keeley gained his great following partially from his strong personality and his ability to convince patients that they could be cured.*

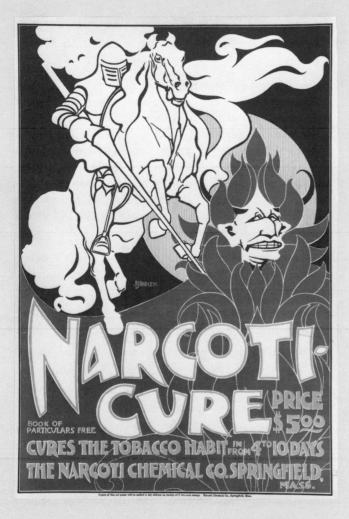

■ This ca. 1895 handbill for Narcoti-Cure, made by the Narcoti Chemical Company of Springfield, Massachusetts, reflected Americans' growing concern regarding tobacco smoking. Many physicians considered tobacco a narcotic because it produced relaxation and addiction. Hence, the name of this particular cure seemed apt. Popular theories of the day also contended that tobacco robbed the body of nerve energy, making the smoker susceptible to various illnesses and debility.

■ Some physicians and enterprising businessmen believed that a cure for chemical dependencies lay in the natural world, such as Scotch Oats Essence. After all, if scientists were able to isolate and extract powerful drugs such as morphine and cocaine from plants, then it seemed logical that the antidotes for those drugs lay hidden in nature, too. The catalogue advertising the product claimed that "snugly wrapped up in each little kernel of the oat is hidden away a little particle of avenesca, that, now that human skill has found it and extracted it, proves itself to be "that very vegetable tonic that best builds up, nourishes, and restores to health, vigor and natural tone the exhausted brain and weakened nerves."

■ *Opiate addiction was not unique to the United States. The problem was also widespread in parts of Great Britain and Western Europe. In 1897, French artist Eugene Grasset portrayed the anguish of withdrawal in his lithograph, "The Morphine Addict." The physical distress of withdrawal symptoms was matched only by the emotional fear addicts experienced when faced with deprivation of their drug. This physiological and psychological dependence convinced many doctors and the public that opiates were dangerous substances capable of enslaving their users unless controlled by the state or medical profession.* Courtesy, anonymous lender.

drawing them from the drug, as that is the greatest torture I can imagine." As drug historian Wayne Morgan observed, opiate withdrawal was

both physically painful and emotionally exhausting. The patient experienced copious discharges from the mucous membranes, vomiting, and diarrhea. This reduced him to an infantile condition, which heightened his sense of degradation and helplessness. There was sharp pain in the muscles, often seeming to make the bones ache, spasms, and a general sense of aching throughout the body. The skin became hypersensitive. The prick of a needle might feel like impalement, or crucifixion, as the more florid addict-memorists said.[22]

As the addicts' withdrawal continued, their craving for opium intensified, and many patients never overcame the agonizing desire for the drug. After the initial symptoms passed, the patient experienced chills, loss of appetite, insomnia, and deep depression.

Doctors disagreed on the best way to ease a patient through opiate withdrawal. Germany's Dr. Edouard Levinstein advocated a harsh regime in the late 1870s whereby opiates were withdrawn abruptly, cold turkey—so called because during withdrawal patients experienced waves of goose flesh which made the skin resemble that of a plucked, cold turkey. An alternate approach withdrew patients gradually from opiates or alcohol using ever smaller doses of the drug, combined with sedative hypnotics such as chloral to allay withdrawal symptoms. Patients received soothing baths, massages, electrical shock, and other therapies. D. F. MacMartin, a lawyer and morphine addict, endorsed this approach, saying, "The only logical cure for morphinism is the gradual reduction system."[23] A third technique included the administration of other drugs. In the

1880s, physicians hoped that cocaine might cure alcoholism and opiate addiction; they similarly used cannabis, codeine, and then heroin to ease withdrawal symptoms, often finding that the patient had developed a craving for the cure. Despite the efforts of the medical community, the number of successful cures for alcoholism and opiate addiction remained dismally low. When it became apparent that modern medical science offered little hope, many Americans began to believe that the solution to drug problems lay in laws that would control drug use, reform society, and ensure the common good.

NOTES

1. Cynthia Palmer and Michael Horowitz, *Shaman Woman, Mainline Lady,* (New York: Quill, 1982), 63.

2. H. Wayne Morgan, *Drugs in America: A Social History, 1800–1980,* (Syracuse: Syracuse University Press, 1981), 15.

3. Morgan, *Drugs,* 24.

4. Thomas De Quincey, *The Confessions of an English Opium Eater,* (Boston: Ticknor and Field, 1859), 66–67.

5. Edward Brecher, *Licit and Illicit Drugs,* (Boston: Little, Brown and Company, 1972), 312–13, 317.

6. "A Growing Metropolitan Evil," *Frank Leslie's Illustrated Newspaper* (12 May 1883), 190, discusses how opium smoking spread from upper class women to working class women.

7. Palmer and Horowitz, *Shaman,* 71–77.

8. Ari Hoogenboom and Olive Hoogenboom, *The Gilded Age,* (Englewood Cliffs, N.J.: Prentice Hall, Inc., 1967), 139.

9. *Scientific American* 7 August 1880, 84.

10. *Harper's Weekly* 9 July 1859, 434. Statistics for beer consumption taken from Mark Lender and James Kirby Martin, *Drinking in America,* (New York: Free Press, 1982), 196.

11. Jack S. Blocker, Jr., *"Give to the Wind Thy Fears": The Women's Temperance Crusade, 1873–1874,* (Westport, Conn.: Greenwood Press, 1985), 97, 57.

12. Joseph Fleischman, *The Art of Blending and Compounding Liquors and Wines,* (New York: Dick and Fitzgerald, 1885), 12–13.

13. *Illustrated History of American Eating and Dining,* (American Heritage Publishing Company, 1964), 61–62.

14. Perry Duis, *The Saloon: Public Drinking in Chicago and Boston, 1880–1920.* (Urbana: University of Chicago Press, 1983), 47.

15. R. Vashon Rogers, Jr., *Drinks, Drinkers, and Drinking: or the Law and History of Intoxicating Liquors,* (1881; reprint, Littleton, Colo.: Fred B. Rothman and Company, 1985), 154.

16. Blocker, *Give to the Winds Thy Fears,* 210.

17. Edward Turner, *The History of the First Inebriate Asylum in the World,* (New York: Edward Turner, 1888), 68.

18. Turner, *History,* 75.

19. A. L. Worcester, *Knowledge Applied: A Valuable Collection of Practical Receipts,* (Philadelphia: Greene and Company, 1868), 300–301.

20. Otto L. Bettmann, *The Good Old Days—They Were Terrible,* (New York: Random House, 1974), 133.

21. Turner, *History,* 184.

22. Morgan, *Drugs,* 66, 69–70.

23. Daniel Frederick MacMartin, *Thirty Years in Hell: or The Confessions of a Drug Fiend,* (Topeka, Kans.: Capper Printing Co., 1921), 82.

PUCK.

THE AGE OF DRUGS.

SALOON KEEPER. — The kind of drunkard I make is going out of fashion. I can't begin to compete with this fellow.

4

REGULATION AND REACTION

1900–1956

I n the late nineteenth and early twentieth centuries, many reformers crusaded for drug regulation as part of a broader, cultural movement to create a modern, progressive society. The ever-spiralling complexity of large corporations and modern industrial life convinced many Americans that they needed federal laws to safeguard the public good. As immigration increased, some Americans believed that the public needed protection not only from the exploitation of big business, but also from ethnic and racial groups. Fears that these groups might threaten the status quo sometimes distorted or magnified popular perceptions of a particular group's use of alcohol and other drugs. Ironically, the very legislation that regulated one drug often caused some Americans to turn to another.

REGULATION: OPIATES AND COCAINE

Dr. Harvey W. Wiley of the U. S. Department of Agriculture led the campaign to regulate the patent medicine industry in particular and the quality of food and drugs in general. Under his guidance, journalist and muck-raker Samuel Adams Hopkins exposed the patent medicine industry in the popular magazine, *Collier's*. Author Sinclair Lewis raised yet another alarm in his novel, *The Jungle*, which portrayed the unsanitary and unsavory practices of an American slaughterhouse and meat packer. As a result of such

■ Puck *satirized the casual and widespread use of drugs with this cartoon published around 1900. The barkeeper, casting a disgruntled look at the druggist of the "Killem Quick Pharmacy," mutters "The kind of drunkard I make is going out of fashion." While the druggist dispenses a bottle of bracer, probably an alcoholic concoction of some sort, children help themselves to soothing syrups laced with opium. Cocaine, opium, arsenic, strychnine, and morphine sit neatly on the counter.*

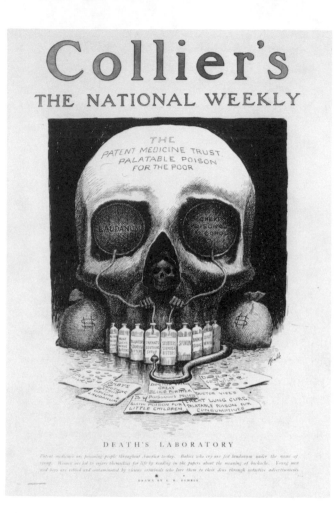

Collier's
THE NATIONAL WEEKLY

THE
PATENT MEDICINE TRUST.
PALATABLE POISON
FOR THE POOR

LAUDANUM

DEATH'S LABORATORY

■ *Grisly and sensational images such as this one published by the popular magazine* Collier's *June 3, 1905, made many Americans take a closer look at their medicine cabinets—and led to the passage of the Pure Food and Drug Act of 1906. Consumption of medicines containing opiates and cocaine dropped by about 30 percent after companies were forced to list product contents on package labels. Many companies, such as the proprietor of Mrs. Winslow's Soothing Syrup, resisted the law at first and refused to list the ingredients accurately. Dogged investigations, public hearings, and negative publicity finally brought the syrup manufacturer and other firms to heel.*

books and articles and of the efforts of Dr. Wiley, the Pure Food and Drug Act, known as the Wiley law, went into effect in 1906.

The law required manufacturers to list a product's ingredients on its label. No longer could patent medicine companies simply peddle secret formulas and miracle cures containing habit-forming drugs that might addict unsuspecting customers. Many mothers who once happily bought soothing syrups for teething infants, recoiled from such products when their morphine or opium bases appeared on package labels.

It was the recreational use of cocaine and opiates, however, that alarmed most citizens. Reformers and newspapers charged that a lack of federal regulation spawned a large population of addicts. Some claimed that as many as one million Americans suffered from addiction. While it is difficult to ascertain an exact figure, historian David Musto suggests that addiction rates peaked in 1900 at two to four hundred thousand people. "What actually increased," he concludes, "was the fear directed at addiction by officials and the public."[1] In addition, unreasoning fears about ethnic groups also translated into fears about drug use. Reporters fueled the growing hysteria with lurid tales about African Americans' use of cocaine. One, for example, alleged that cocaine turned black men into bulletproof, sex-crazed sharpshooters. In fact, a small percentage of people, both black and white, did use cocaine. Ironically, cocaine was popular in Southern states that restricted or prohibited alcohol partly because of the old conviction that liquor might stir unrest among African Americans. Peddlers sold cocaine

"Before you do another thing *James*, bring me a CLUB COCKTAIL I'm so tired shopping make it a MARTINI." I need a little Tonic and it's so much better than a drug of any kind"

FOR SALE BY ALL DEALERS.

G. F. HEUBLEIN & BRO.

HARTFORD. NEW YORK. LONDON.

door to door, and cocaine joints operated in large cities such as Atlanta. The truth of the matter was that there was no proof to indicate that African Americans used the substance more than whites; indeed, medical evidence gathered from hospitals and asylums pointed to the opposite conclusion.[2]

Concern about opium intensified after 1898 when the United States gained control of the

■ *This ca. 1910 Danish poster promoted a novel about an aristocratic morphine addict. At the time, both in Europe and the United States, the prospect that the very people who led society, government, and commerce might be engaged in recreational drug use sent a scintillating chill through the public. Exploiting the general anxiety about drug use, American newspapers and tabloids such as the* New York Herald *and* San Francisco Examiner *ran sensational stories about young wealthy upper class matrons who reputedly purchased gold plated syringes in diamond studded cases.*

MORFINISTEN

■ *Some liquor companies cleverly used the turn-of-the-century drug scare to great advantage. Few people recognized ethyl alcohol as a drug. The nineteenth-century belief that a cocktail was simply a healthful tonic or pick-me-up triumphed and prevailed as the popularity of Dover's Powders, laudanum, and coca wines declined. Club Cocktail, the subject of this 1902 advertisement published in* Harper's Weekly, *was a premixed, ready-to-pour cocktail. Customers could purchase bottled Martini, Manhattan, and Old Fashion cocktails to keep on hand.*

Philippine Islands, where opium use was endemic. Some Americans, like the first Episcopal bishop of the Philippines, Charles Henry Brent, believed America had a moral duty to abolish the opium trade. Americans feared that servicemen stationed on the islands would return home addicted to opium. In addition, American traders protested that the silver bullion with which the Chinese bought British-Indian opium could be better spent on American goods. Abolition of the opium trade promised new markets for America. Another factor underlying the increased concern over the opium trade was the long-standing hostility towards Chinese immigrants who competed for American jobs—and who smoked opium. Racial hostility climaxed after several sensational and public beatings of Chinese travelers and immigrants, and around 1904 Congress voted to exclude all Chinese laborers. China retaliated with an embargo on American goods. In spite of these differences, both China and the United States wished to eradicate opium addiction under their jurisdictions. President Theodore Roosevelt, eager for the United States to assume a world leadership role and to mend fences with China, called for a conference at Shanghai to discuss international control of the opium trade. In 1909, Congress banned the importation of opium for smoking. Other international conferences on opium control followed at The Hague in 1911 and 1912.

While pressing for international controls, the United States needed a drug regulation policy of its own. Lawmakers' efforts resulted in the Harrison Narcotics Act of 1914, with which they intended to regulate the medical use of opiates and cocaine while eliminating their nonmedical use. The Harrison Narcotics Act licensed doctors, manufacturers, importers, and distributors who handled the drugs and required them to keep detailed records of all transactions. Although cocaine is a stimulant, rather than a narcotic drug that induces sleep, legislators included cocaine with the narcotics opium, morphine, heroin, and codeine. The act allowed physicians to prescribe these drugs "in pursuit of professional practice only" and many physicians con-

■ *President Woodrow Wilson and the Democratic party supported the regulation of opiates and cocaine. In this cartoon, "The Dope Fiends," published by* Puck *in 1914, President Wilson holds aloft a bottle labeled morphine tariff and assures the panicked gathering, "Don't be alarmed, gentlemen. We won't take it from you all at once. We'll taper you down gradually, and after a while, you'll have enough confidence in yourselves to get along without it." The tax levied by the Harrison Narcotics Act was a modest one. Doctors and druggists paid one dollar a year for the tax stamp that allowed them to prescribe the drugs. But weaning addicts off of opiates proved to be more difficult than the drafters of the act ever envisioned.* Courtesy, William Helfand.

THE DOPE-FIENDS.

Dr. WILSON—Don't be alarmed, gentlemen. We won't take it from you all at once. We'll taper you down gradually, and after a while you'll have confidence enough in yourselves to get along without it.

■ *The New York City police confiscated this heroin label, along with the drug itself around 1920. Just like today, drug dealers marketed different brands of heroin whose name or packaging made them appealing to customers. Some people referred to heroin as horse because of this brand.* Courtesy, New York Police Academy Museum.

tinued to prescribe drugs for their addicted patients. In the early twentieth century, however, drug addiction was not classified as a disease. Consequently, the Supreme Court later decreed in 1919 that doctors could not lawfully prescribe drugs to maintain addicts because they were not technically sick. The addict became a criminal; the doctor, an accomplice. Doctors, who for years had administered maintenance level doses to addicts, suddenly faced criminal prosecution. *American Medicine* protested: "The addict is denied the medical care he urgently needs, open, above-board sources from which he formerly obtained his drug supply are closed to him, and he is driven to the underworld where he can get his drug. . . ."[3] A number of physicians who continued

to prescribe maintenance drugs for dependent patients were arrested and jailed.

As a result of the Harrison Narcotics Act, some Americans with lesser degrees of dependency simply stopped using drugs; some individuals switched to other drugs such as barbiturates. Large cities such as New York opened clinics to provide drugs and temporary care for addicts awaiting admission to hospitals for withdrawal treatment. The clinics were intended to reduce suffering and prevent the growth of a black market in drugs. But skeptics argued that many clients had no desire to be cured of their addictions and that the clinics were simply maintaining addicts in violation of the Supreme Court's 1919 ruling. One by one, the forty-four public narcotics clinics closed, driving many addicts to underground sources and to unscrupulous doctors, who for the right price, wrote prescriptions for the addicted.

By the 1920s, the profile of the opiate user had changed drastically. In 1900, the average opium addict was likely to be a white, middle class, middle-aged female who took relatively inexpensive patent medicines or prescribed opiates such as Dover's Powders. Doctors recommended these preparations to women complaining of headaches, nervousness, and anxiety. The patients were unaware of the drugs addictive properties. The Pure Food and Drug Act of 1906 and the Harrison Narcotics Act gradually weaned many men and women off of addictive medications and prevented the start of new addictions among working and middle class consumers. On the other hand, the Harrison Narcotics Act and subsequent legislation,

■ *M. M. Haeusermann and Company made this chromolithographed picture for the Thixton, Millett distillery in 1904, probably as an advertising piece for a saloon or taproom. To a society that was becoming rapidly urban and industrial, this vignette of the preindustrial past was especially appealing. Those were the days when whiskey remained untaxed and unrestricted, when customers simply hauled themselves and their jugs to the local distiller, in this case, none other than the rugged American folk hero, Daniel Boone, the personification of freedom. Forgotten were concerns of adulterated or green, unaged liquor.*

as author Erich Goode asserts, fostered "the emergence of a criminal class of addicts—*a criminal class that had not existed previously.* The link between addiction and crime—the view that the addict was by definition a criminal—was forged." As Goode further observes,

Probably the most important contribution that law enforcement had made to the problem of addiction is

■ *This photograph captured a moment at the home of Emil and Katherine Fleig in Rochester, New York, around 1905. The Fleigs lived in a German neighborhood. Emil and his friends are shown here enjoying beer from Rochester's Moerlbach Brewing Company. Katherine Fleig, holding an empty glass, watches shyly from the back steps. Many immigrants had very different attitudes towards alcohol than those of temperance leaders and Anti-Saloon Leaguers. These attitudes dominated among immigrants from Italy, Germany, and Eastern Europe, where alcoholism rates were low and where beer and wine, not distilled alcohol, were more popular. Many people viewed wine and beer simply as food, part of any good meal, and considered temperance claims to the contrary to be silly and extreme.* Courtesy, Alan Mueller.

the *creation of an addict subculture. . . . It was the criminalization of addiction that created addicts as a special and distinctive group, and it is the subcultural aspect of addicts that gives them their recruiting power.*[4]

The Harrison Narcotics Act also indirectly led to the rise of a black market. Opiates, once inexpensive and easy to obtain, became scarce, expensive, and highly profitable for those engaging in an illicit narcotics trade. One addict recalled,

After the Harrison Act, heroin became increasingly hard and expensive to get. It created a black market. . . . The Italians were involved in the beginning, and the drugstores were involved in the beginning. There was one drugstore that gave us Christmas presents. It was really something: a brand-new, shining hypodermic needle with a little ribbon around it and a little card, "Merry Christmas."[5]

To suppress the black market, Congress fortified the Harrison Narcotics Act, in 1924, by prohibiting the importation of crude opium used in manufacturing heroin. As the domestic heroin supply dwindled, smuggled heroin became a more lucrative trade. More potent and compact than opium, heroin was easier to transport and to conceal. Dealers then cut, or diluted, the heroin many times with milk sugar and other adulterants and resold it at a high profit. Heroin became common in city slums, traditionally the scene of gambling, prostitution, and gangs. Some gang members dealt in drugs to earn fast money and initiated young inner city males into drug use.[6]

REGULATION OF ALCOHOL

The same spirit of reform that sought to regulate opiates, cocaine, and tobacco, did not ignore its old adversary, alcohol. The Anti-Saloon League, founded in 1895, worked diligently to pass county legislation prohibiting local alcohol sales. By 1913, almost 50 percent of all Americans lived under some sort of prohibitionary law, and many congressmen won their seats by backing the Anti-Saloon League's platform. Encouraged by this success, league mem-

■ *At first glance, the sword-bearing evangelist on this poster printed for the Ohio Dry Convention in 1917 might appear to be an American Joan of Arc. She was, in fact, the figure of Justice, a logical emblem for the Anti-Saloon League which had absorbed a broader group, the Citizens' Law and Order League. Both leagues were passionately concerned with the relationship between liquor and crime. They were particularly troubled by the number of poor city youths who drank heavily and who consequently fell into trouble with the law. To save the youths and to solve other problems, they campaigned actively for local and state laws prohibiting liquor sales to minors and, eventually, for national prohibition.*

DRUGS AND THE SILVER SCREEN

After the Harrison Narcotics Act, opiate and cocaine use declined, but its recreational use continued among some Hollywood actors and actresses. In 1922, *Vanity Fair* reported, "Drugs are not as much in evidence as during the more trying days of winter, but they still spread their genial influence around at some of the more exclusive functions. Last week Lulu Lenore . . . gave a small house dance for the younger addicts. 'Will you come to my Snow-Ball?' read the clever invitations. . . . Otho Everard kept the company in a roar as he dispensed little packages of cocaine, morphine, and heroin."[1] A number of films spoofed cocaine sniffing and opium smoking, such as *The Mystery of the Leaping Fish* (1916) in which Douglas Fairbanks, Sr. played detective Coke Ennyday, a spin-off of Sherlock Holmes. But after a rash of drug related scandals and deaths, including that of matinee idol Wallace Reid in 1923, Hollywood blackballed known drug users and censored the portrayal of drug use on screen.

Smoking opium, or hop, was associated with money, theater and movie stars, and the fast set in the 1920s. One opium smoker, or pipie, recalled her own experiences smoking hop in New York: "I started going to parties. They had a lot of big stars that were on opium. They'd put a mattress on the floor. They wore beautiful silk pajamas and had a big can of opium and a pipe. . . . We had dishes for all sorts of fruits and candies—hard candies, in case you got dry from smoking."[2]

NOTES

1. Michael Starks, *Cocaine Fiends and Reefer Madness*, (East Brunswick, N.J.: Cornwall Books, 1982), 46.

2. David Courtwright, *Addicts Who Survived,* (Knoxville: The University of Tennessee Press, 1989), 80-81.

■ *World War I and the 1920s drastically changed everyday life and social values. Along with the right to vote, bobbed hair, and short skirts, the modern woman took up smoking. Manufacturers encouraged the trend with advertisements showing romantic scenes in which men and women smoked. Perhaps Lucky cigarettes launched the most persuasive campaign in 1930 with ads that promoted cigarettes as dieting aids. "We do not say smoking Luckies reduces flesh. We do say that when tempted to over-indulge, 'Reach for a Lucky instead.'"*

SMOKE SIGNALS

Some Americans rejected tobacco, believing it was a narcotic drug. As cigarette sales steadily climbed in the early twentieth century, concerned citizens organized anticigarette leagues, closely aligned to temperance groups, such as the Anti-Saloon League. Both kinds of groups believed the traditional nineteenth-century wisdom that tobacco stimulated thirst, thus tempting smokers to drink alcohol. As a temperance leader had earlier warned, "The non-user of alcohol—if he is a tobacco user, is standing upon slippery ground."[1] Inventor Thomas Edison who relished a good cigar but dismissed any employee caught smoking cigarettes, argued that, unlike a cigar or pipe of tobacco, "the cigarette has a violent action in the nerve centers, producing degeneration of the cells of the brain, which is quite rapid among boys. Unlike most narcotics, this degeneration is permanent and uncontrollable. I employ no person who smokes cigarettes."[2]

By 1921, some states prohibited cigarettes or restricted their purchase. Despite such laws, cigarette sales soared from 45.6 billion in 1918 to 118.6 billion in 1929.[3] Advertisements and Hollywood movies portrayed the modern, stylish, and successful woman as a smoker, which convinced more women to light up.

NOTES

1. Thomas Deering, *Intemperance,* (New York: Cowan and Co., 1870), 91.

2. Edward Brecher, *Licit and Illicit Drugs*, (Boston: Little, Brown and Company, 1972), 230.

3. Erich Goode, *Drugs in American Society*, (New York: McGraw Hill, 1989), 206.

bers such as Wayne Wheeler, Purley A. Baker, and Earnest Cherrington began to organize a national prohibition movement. They enlisted churches as "out posts" of the campaign and distributed free posters, leaflets, and suggestions for sermons. The distilling industry and brewers responded feebly; they were ultimately ineffective because they lacked a cooperative spirit. Many brewers naively believed that temperance leaders sought only to prohibit hard liquor. Believing beer to be a healthful, nourishing, and harmless beverage, brewers could not foresee that beer might be targeted for prohibition too. Brewers thus disassociated themselves from the distilling industry, confident that the distiller's loss would be the brewer's gain.

In December 1917, Congress approved the Eighteenth Amendment which prohibited alcohol production, sales, and distribution. Unlike narcotics, alcohol possession alone was not considered a criminal offense. While the Eighteenth Amendment was undergoing ratification by the states, prohibitionists used the conditions created by World War I to advantage. They argued that drinking was unpatriotic because it diverted grains needed for food by the American and Allied forces. Consequently, Congress passed the Lever Food and Fuel Control Act in 1917 which prohibited alcohol production but not sales of existing stocks. The law remained in effect after the armistice was signed in November 1918 because the armistice did not itself produce an official peace treaty. Anticipating that the Eighteenth Amendment would be adopted, Congress enacted the Volstead Act in 1919, named after Representative Andrew Volstead of Minnesota who rewrote and presented the bill. While the Eighteenth Amendment outlawed intoxicating liquors, the Volstead Act was its enabling legislation, defining intoxicating liquors as those containing more than 0.5 percent alcohol. The Volstead Act also regulated the use of sacramental wines and allowed physicians to prescribe liquor for medicinal purposes—sending a steady stream of "patients" to their doctors. The Eighteenth Amendment, or Prohibition, was ratified immediately and went into effect in January 1920.

Prohibition decreased alcohol consumption, the number of alcohol related illnesses, and deaths from cirrhosis. The law and the high price of illegal alcohol discouraged many; a quart of Scotch that cost two dollars before Prohibition sold for ten dollars after its passage. But while thousands stopped drinking, others did not. Drinking was so deeply interwoven into the fabric of social life and custom, that many Americans simply ignored or circumvented the law. Plenty of illicit liquor was available for those who sought it. The rich and resourceful stockpiled wine and liquor prior to 1920. New York's Governor Franklin D. Roosevelt, for example, continued to serve Martinis in his office every day at four o'clock, much to his wife's displeasure. Wineries, such as the Widmer winery of Naples, New York, sold bottled grape juice with a label warning that fermentation would occur if yeast and sugar were accidently added to the juice. Enterprising citizens made their own beer and wine while the astute, particularly in rural areas, stoked up stills made from copper plumbing supplies. But it was in the large cities where Americans most

readily found alcohol. As historian Mark Lender noted, cities offered the largest pool of potential customers for illicit alcohol and the transportation and distribution networks necessary to supply them. Moreover, an urban culture developed fostering new ideas about government, personal liberty, women's emancipation, and family life that challenged the traditional values espoused by the Anti-Saloon League. Cities such as New York, Chicago, and

■ *Around 1934, artist Ben Shahn painted this gouache, "Delivering barrels and boxes, alley scene between two brownstones," intended for a mural project at the fashionable nightclub, The Central Park Casino. The painting portrayed some of the ironies of Prohibition. Whether intended for the respectable upper class or the speakeasy, liquor came out of the same illicit still. Whereas money shielded one group from the harsh realities of organized crime, poorer citizens were more likely to become its victims. Here a portrait of gangster Al Capone faces a mural of the Sons of Temperance.* Courtesy, Museum of the City of New York, permanent deposit of the Whitney Museum of American Art.

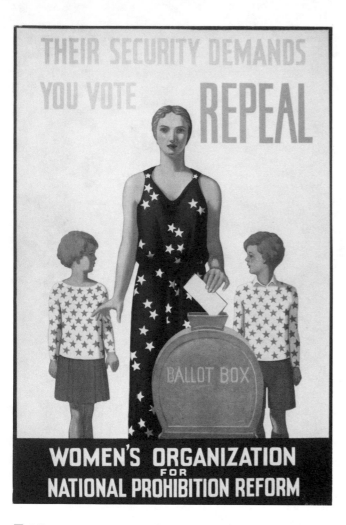

THEIR SECURITY DEMANDS YOU VOTE REPEAL

WOMEN'S ORGANIZATION FOR NATIONAL PROHIBITION REFORM

BALLOT BOX

■ *This 1932 poster portrays the American mother safeguarding her children. It was a familiar theme to Americans, presented here with a new twist. Unlike earlier posters published by the WCTU and Anti-Saloon League that depicted mothers protecting their children from the saloon and the evils of liquor, here a mother and franchised citizen casts her vote to repeal Prohibition, a law that many viewed as a violation of civil liberties. Other groups, including the Women's Organization for National Prohibition Reform, blamed Prohibition for the wave of crime and homicide that characterized the era.*

Detroit spawned large numbers of speakeasies or illegal bars where patrons gained entrance by whispering a password or flashing special admittance cards. Some speakeasies, like New York's Twenty-One Club, served excellent food and imported liquor to its wealthy and upper middle class clientele, but most operated out of a back room or basement.

The Eighteenth Amendment became a nightmare to enforce. Prohibition agents, the Dry Flyers, even took to the skies to spot illicit country stills and trucks smuggling alcohol across the Canadian border. The federal government's Prohibition Unit initially estimated it would cost $5 million to implement the law; it requested $28 million in 1923, and by the end of Prohibition, $300 million.[7] More agents chased lawbreakers, and penalties against them escalated without great effect. As soon as officials closed one speakeasy down, another would spring up nearby. By 1929, the New York City police commissioner estimated that there were thirty-two thousand speakeasies in the city alone.[8]

The quality of bootleg liquor varied because it was produced without any safety standards enforced by states or federal governments. Some dealers obtained imported or good quality domestic whiskey, brandy, and gin. Others offered cocktails concocted from all sorts of flavorings that disguised the taste of their bathtub gin base. The latter earned its name from the way it was made. Bootleggers mixed alcohol, juniper flavoring, and glycerine together in large bottles that could fit only under a bathtub spigot which provided water, the final ingredient. Less scrupulous or sloppy dealers "washed" industrial denatured alcohol to remove its poisonous additives. Sometimes bootleggers accidentally produced methyl alcohol, a potion that led to blindness or death. Wine and beer were bulky, difficult to ship, and hard to store discreetly, making them more expensive. Thus, many beer and wine drinkers switched to distilled liquors instead.

Some Americans living in large cities such as New York and New Orleans found another alternative to alcohol, marijuana, known as tea, muggles, or weed. Travelers and journalists periodically reported a limited, recreational use of marijuana in Kentucky, Southern states, and along the Mexican border during the nineteenth and early twentieth centuries. More Americans used marijuana, however, after alcohol became illegal. Some dealers discovered that marijuana was cheaper and easier to distribute than liquor; whereas a cocktail in a speakeasy could cost seventy-five cents, a quarter bought one or two reefers, or marijuana cigarettes. Users frequented tea pads, places similar to speakeasies where they could buy and smoke the drug, which, at the time of Prohibition, was not illegal. The ports of New York and, particularly, New Orleans provided a convenient entry route for marijuana from Tampic and Vera Cruz in Mexico and Havana. From New Orleans, where blues musicians gained a reputation for smoking the weed, dealers carried marijuana up the Mississippi and places beyond, even as far north as Cleveland, Ohio.

Perhaps the most serious consequence of Prohibition was the increase in organized crime and in homicide rates. Profits made from illicit liquor helped gangs extend their operations in drug dealing, prostitution, gambling, and violence. Some gangs, like the one headed by Chicago's Al Capone, grew into well-organized syndicates. As rival gangs waged war on each other for control of the liquor trade, police and innocent citizens were caught in the cross fire. Despite these problems, Irving Fisher, an outspoken supporter of Prohibition argued, "Prohibition has already accomplished incalculable good, hygienically, economically, and socially. Real personal liberty, the liberty to give and enjoy the full use of our faculties, is increased by Prohibition." But by the late 1920s, Fisher's arguments sounded lame. Violence and the sharply rising homicide rate led to a reevaluation of Prohibition. If the saloon was a threat to the home, then the illicit liquor trade was even worse. Some concluded that a legalized liquor industry would thwart crime syndicates by removing their item of trade and would help restore law and order to communities. This concern for public safety triggered one of the arguments for repeal of Prohibition.

Individual liberty was another argument. Attorney Clarence Darrow, an outspoken opponent of Prohibition, protested that "Prohibition is an outrageous and senseless invasion of the personal liberty of millions of intelligent and temperate persons who see nothing dangerous or immoral in the moderate consumption of alcoholic beverages."[9]

A number of other forces conspired to take the initiative away from Prohibitionists. Factious infighting splintered the Anti-Saloon League which had brought the Noble Experiment about in the first place, and the group gradually lost its financial and political base. A new group of "crusaders" actively campaigned for repeal of the Eighteenth Amendment, claiming that it violated civil liberties and drained taxpayers' purses. As the nation entered the Great Depression, the possibility of

new jobs and new revenues from a revitalized liquor industry further strengthened the arguments for the repeal of Prohibition. On December 5, 1933, President Franklin Roosevelt signed the Twenty-First Amendment officially repealing Prohibition. The Noble Experiment was over; prohibition of another drug was about to begin.

REGULATION: MARIJUANA

In 1930, the narcotics division of the Prohibition Unit was reorganized as the Federal Bureau of Narcotics under Harry J. Anslinger. His approach towards drug control was direct and matter-of-fact, stating "The answer to the problem is simple—get rid of drugs, pushers and users. Period."[10] Throughout his career, Anslinger lobbied steadily for stricter policies and more stringent penalties for drug dealers and drug users. The Uniform Narcotics Drug Act of 1932, backed by Anslinger, represented a move in that direction. Until the passage of the act, many states had contradictory laws concerning narcotic drugs; in some states, enforcement was lax or sometimes arbitrary. The legislation

BECOME A PERFECT HOST
in 12 Easy Lessons

Here are the twelve most popular mixed drinks. The perfect host should know them all—and they are all he really needs to know to please his guests.

■ *Cocktail tables, liquor cabinets, and other drinking accessories were trendy home furnishings once repeal legalized drinking. The five-to-seven-o'clock cocktail party became an important social ritual suited to the smaller, servantless homes and apartments many Americans now occupied. The cocktail party offered a convenient way to entertain large numbers of guests in small spaces without providing individual seating or dinner. Nevertheless, rules of etiquette developed for dress and behavior, including the serving of finger foods, which allowed hosts and guests to snack gracefully while holding a glass in one hand.*

■ *As one cocktail recipe book asserted, "Half the fun of casual drinking is lost if you mix your cocktails in the kitchen." Although the task might be more sensibly done in a kitchen, shaking cocktails in the living room where everyone could watch further ritualized the happy hour. Manufacturers produced a dizzying array of shakers, stirrers, glassware, tongs, trays, measures, and muddlers to accommodate the craze inspired partly by Hollywood and Madison Avenue. Debonair movie stars such as William Powell and Humphrey Bogart and their sophisticated leading ladies used the cocktail as an elegant prop in their films. Americans made cocktails in their homes, thus bringing into the living room a bit of Hollywood's glamour.*

MUGGLES

Although marijuana use was not widespread until the late 1960s, it was available to those who knew where to look for it, as author and drifter Bertha Thompson noted in her 1937 autobiography. She commented, "Marijuana is called among the users, 'muggles'. . . . It came to this country first from Mexico. New Orleans and all the southern cities are full of it. In New Orleans it is grown commonly in the back yards of Old Town. It is available also in every northern city. In south Chicago there is a whole field growing wild, which is harvested by Mexicans and various small wholesale dealers. . . . In almost every city {marijuana cigarettes} may be had as low as twenty-five cents each. In New Orleans, they are two for a quarter."[1]

Similarly, a New York city heroin addict recalled his early experiences with marijuana in 1939. "I started smoking marijuana when I was about seventeen. There was a lot of it in the area, and it was cheap. We used to get seven joints for a dollar. A package of twenty-five cost two dollars. . . . The people who distributed the marijuana were all Puerto Rican and colored. Guys who worked on boats brought it in from Mexico. Then it would go through the vine: one guy would buy a pound and he'd make joints out of it, a thousand joints. A pound used to cost about fifteen dollars, and he'd make about one hundred and fifty dollars on a pound. That's how it got around."[2]

NOTES

1. Cynthia Palmer and Michael Horowitz, *Shaman Woman, Mainline Lady*, (New York: Quill, 1982), 134.

2. David Courtwright, *Addicts Who Survived*, (Knoxville: The University of Tennessee Press, 1989), 226.

■ *This poster, made by Pacific Show Print of Los Angeles, California, advertised the movie,* Marijuana: Weed with Roots in Hell, *a film released in 1937—the year Congress passed the Marijuana Tax Act. A few Hollywood directors saw marijuana as the stuff that box office sales were made of. Taking advantage of the stories surrounding marijuana use at the time, screenwriters wove lurid and melodramatic plots, not unlike the stories depicted in the "Drunkard's Progress" prints of the eighteenth and nineteenth centuries. An individual's introduction to the substance led the innocent down the road to lust, crime, and despair—and in the case of marijuana, Americans believed, to a heroin habit.*

helped to standardize state laws regarding opiates and cocaine, while the control of marijuana became a state's option.

In the early 1930s, outlandish stories existed about the effects of smoking marijuana. Although the drug is not a narcotic, marijuana was misrepresented by the media and federal agencies as a narcotic weed that led to heroin use, insanity, and sex crimes. Hollywood sensationalized the drug in films such as *Marijuana, Assassin of Youth* (1935) and *Reefer Madness* (1936), which later became a classic cult film that inspired young adults to try the drug.

Narcotics Commissioner Anslinger soon joined the fight to regulate marijuana. He acted partly to advance his own antidrug agenda and partly in response to nativist political pressure from Americans in the Southwest where many Mexican immigrant field laborers had earlier settled. As the Great Depression deepened, some Americans resented these immigrants who competed for scarce jobs. Fears focused on the customary use of marijuana among Mexicans. Wild stories abounded claiming that the drug led to homicides, rapes, thefts, and violent crime. Scapegoating Mexicans, Colorado's *Daily Courier* railed, "I wish I could show you what a small marijuana cigarette can do to one of our degenerate Spanish-speaking residents. . . . [M]arijuana has figured in the greatest number of crimes in the past few years."[11] Reports that Southern African Americans were using the drug, shocking stories of crimes committed by marijuana-crazed murderers, and insistent lobbying led to passage of the Marijuana Tax Act in 1937. The law permitted the medical use of marijuana, but made the transfer of marijuana between private citizens illegal without purchase of a transfer tax stamp.

REGULATION: 1950s

During the Second World War, military blockades halted trade from Turkey and Asia making it more difficult to smuggle opiates into the country. Heroin shortages caused panics among users on America's streets. An addict remembered:

There were no drugs in New York during World War II, no drugs in Philadelphia, no drugs in Chicago—there were no drugs on the East Coast. *No drugs.* We traveled around in "wolf packs." Somebody would come up and say, "There's some drugs on Forty-Second Street!" We'd yell, "Taxi! Taxi! Taxi!" Everybody would run down there; as soon as you'd get there, it was out.[12]

In lieu of heroin, people found ways to obtain illegally other opiates such as morphine and paregoric, or they used prescription drugs.

Once peace was declared, heroin reappeared on city streets, although addicts reported that it was more expensive and of lower quality than the prewar product. By the early 1950s, the press again reported a heroin epidemic, particularly in the port city of New York. Newspapers and the media stereotyped the heroin user as a young black or Hispanic male from the ghetto who committed crimes to support his habit. The media warned that drug pushers lurked everywhere and predicted that they soon would invade middle class suburbs ensnaring white youths. As American paranoia regarding Soviet aggression escalated during the early Cold War and the McCarthy era, some Americans suspected that heroin use was all part of a communist plot to undermine national security. "Dope is the real secret weapon of the Kremlin," charged House Representative Norris Paulson, adding, "The narcotics traffic has grown to such proportions under Communist tutelage that it has become an important factor in defending the United States."[13]

In response, the federal government and many state governments stiffened existing drug laws with the Boggs Act of 1951. Testifying before Congress, Commissioner Harry Anslinger stated unequivocally, if incorrectly, that marijuana use led to heroin addiction. He also argued that marijuana and other cannabis products had no medical application and persuaded the editors of the *United States Pharmacopeia* to remove the drug from its official listings of medically sanctioned substances. Although many physicians voiced their disapproval of this deletion, Anslinger's arguments carried the day, and he succeeded in convincing Congress to raise penalties for both heroin and marijuana possession and trafficking. The Boggs Act fixed minimum, mandatory sentencing for all marijuana and narcotic offenses, despite loud protests from the American Bar Association, which claimed that mandatory first sentences were often unfair and ineffective. By the mid-1950s, half of all narcotic arrests involved African Americans, a statistic which reflected both increased drug use by urban African Americans and intensified racial discrimination by narcotics officers. As historian David Courtwright noted, "When the color of the faces in the tenement windows changed, so did the color of the addicts on the street."[14] Impoverished areas or ghettos traditionally harbored gambling, prostitution, and drug dealers who plied their trades with a minimum of interference from police. When the push to enforce narcotics laws came, it was easier, then and now, for police to arrest individuals selling heroin on a ghetto street corner than in the privacy of a suburban home.

Punitive action against drug dealers and users peaked with the Narcotics Control Act of 1956. The law further increased penalties for drug users, provided lengthy, mandatory, minimum sentences, and, in some cases, the death penalty for persons over eighteen convicted of selling heroin to persons under eighteen. The Federal Bureau of Narcotics and its supporters were convinced that by thus raising the stakes, they would discourage a large percentage of drug use once and for all. They did not fully comprehend, however, the compelling nature of addiction. Approximately 95 percent of the individuals convicted of heroin use who were incarcerated or treated at narcotic farms relapsed into old habits once they returned to society.

Efforts at regulation successfully squelched drug use among middle class Americans, but it survived in subcultures and countercultures, among musicians, beats, and city gangs. Some blues and jazz musicians discovered that heroin helped dissolve stage fright and inhibitions, facilitating the flights of improvisation that marked their style. One musician recalled the attraction of heroin:

I was nervous a little because I was aware that the public was out there listening to me. . . . I had to psych myself

TREATMENT

Governmental regulation of drugs profoundly affected the medical treatment of the chemically dependent. By the late nineteenth century, many Americans believed that people addicted to alcohol were sick. But the medical community and other Americans were divided in their opinions regarding those addicted to drugs, particularly opiates. Many thought opiate dependence was a disease, but as different treatments failed to secure lasting cures, and as the field of psychoanalysis developed, a new viewpoint emerged. Some physicians and psychiatrists suggested that both the craving for drugs and the presence of abstinence syndrome or withdrawal resulted from a functional, not organic cause. They argued that addiction was not a physical disease, but a mental and emotional disorder that withdrawal and forced abstinence would eventually cure. This theory helped usher in the 1914 Harrison Narcotics Act and subsequent U. S. Supreme Court rulings that outlawed maintenance. The law also created a dilemma for many physicians who were reluctant to treat addicts for fear of losing medical licenses or facing imprisonment.

The law also burdened a penal system that could not cope with addicted inmates who had special physical needs. Historian David Musto reports that in 1928, "the three federal penitentiaries . . . had a cell capacity of 3,738 . . . they had a population of 7,589. Of the prisoners, about 2,300 were narcotic law violators, of whom 1,600 were addicted."[1]

One solution appeared to be the establishment of federal narcotic farms. At these modified prisons in rural areas, offenders were removed from temptation, withdrawn from drugs, and rehabilitated through work. Congress approved the creation of narcotic farms in 1929, but the first at Lexington, Kentucky, did not open until 1935. This approach, like other treatment programs, had a dismal success rate. Ninety percent of the patients relapsed into drug use. As one inmate summarized, "But when you're confined it's very different than when you hit that street. You have no direction when you come out of the hospital. While you're in the hospital, you have something to do. . . . You're withdrawing from drugs; that's your main purpose there. When you go out, if you don't have a definite purpose, the time before you start somewhere is problem time, because you're still thinking about drugs."[2]

In contrast to treatment for narcotic addiction, treatment for alcohol dependency advanced in the early twentieth century, although Prohibition actually blocked some studies. The Research Council on Problems of Alcohol formed in 1938 to raise monies for medical research, followed by the establishment of the Yale University Center of Alcohol Studies. The Yale center began the *Quarterly Journal of Studies on Alcohol*, now *The Journal of Studies on Alcohol*. The National Committee for Education on Alcoholism formed in 1944, later renamed the National Council on Alcoholism. Willmar State Hospital in Minnesota developed the twelve step or Minnesota Model for alcoholism, derived from the self-help therapy of the Alcoholics Anonymous's Twelve Steps to Recovery Program. In 1949, Hazelden and a number of other treatment centers were founded to assist the recovering alcoholic. Ironically, just as Dr. E. M. Jellinek, director of the Yale center, popularized the disease concept of alcoholism in the early 1950s, the most punitive narcotics laws were going into effect.

NOTES

1. David Musto, *The American Disease Origins of Narcotic Control,* (New York: Oxford University Press, 1987), 204.

2. David Courtwright, *Addicts Who Survived,* (Knoxville: The University of Tennessee Press, 1989), 301.

up more or less to do it. But if you had some heroin in you, you were ready. At all times . . . the heroin took away the stage fright. In fact, it was almost a must to have some. I think that was the major inducement for so many jazz musicians to use it.[15]

Beside musicians and entertainers, the beats, or beatniks, a nonconformist group viewed by many with suspicion, also began using various drugs. These unconventional social critics, writers, artists, and philosophers of the 1950s were thoroughly disillusioned with postwar society. Seeking excitement and freedom from traditional values, they turned to Eastern philosophy, sexuality, music, and drugs. Jack Kerouac, Allen Ginsberg, and William S. Burroughs wrote frankly on these subjects and introduced them to America's youth. In 1954, Aldous Huxley wrote *Doors of Perception* in which he described his experiences with the hallucinogen, mescaline. "What the rest of us see only under the influence of mescaline," Huxley wrote, "the artist is congenitally equipped to see all the time. His perception is not limited to what is biologically or socially useful."[16] Like De Quincey before him, Huxley wrote that the drug liberated the emotions and senses, literally opening new doors to self-discovery, sensory perception, and knowledge. Huxley's words would influence greatly young adults of the 1960s and would help usher in a new age of drug use and toleration.

NOTES

1. David Musto, *The American Disease Origins of Narcotic Control,* (New York: Oxford University Press, 1987), 282.

2. Ibid., 5–8.

3. Edward Brecher, *Licit and Illicit Drugs,* (Boston: Little, Brown and Company, 1972), 50–51.

4. Erich Goode, *Drugs in American Society,* (New York: McGraw Hill, 1989), 234.

5. David Courtwright, *Addicts Who Survived* (Knoxville: The University of Tennessee Press, 1989), 289–90.

6. David Musto, "Opium, Cocaine and Marijuana in American History," *Scientific American*, July 1991, 40–47.

7. Mark Lender and James Kirby Martin, *Drinking in America*, (New York: Free Press, 1982), 154.

8. Richard Hooker, *Food and Drink in America,* (New York: The Bobbs-Merrill Compnay, Inc., 1981), 304.

9. Lender, *Drinking*, 155.

10. Courtwright, *Addicts*, 12.

11. Musto, *Disease*, 223.

12. Courtwright, *Addicts*, 107.

13. James Vaus, *The Inside Story of Narcotics*, (Grand Rapids, Mich.: Aondervan Publishing Company, 1953), 43.

14. Courtwright, *Addicts*, 17.

15. Ibid., 234.

16. Aldous Huxley, *The Doors of Perception* (New York: Harper and Row, 1956), 33.

Hollywood had banned the portrayal of stories about narcotics from the silver screen in the late 1920s, but To the Ends of the Earth, *starring Dick Powell, broke that rule in 1948, followed by* The Man with the Golden Arm, *with Frank Sinatra, eight years later. After 1956, movie studios agreed that the topic could be treated as long as drug addiction or drug trafficking was shown in a negative light. The agreement opened the door for many films about heroin addiction, such as* The Pusher, *advertised by this lobby card in 1959. Courtesy, International Museum of Photography at George Eastman House.*

5

THE DRUG CULTURE
1960–1990s

The pendulum that had swung towards rigid conservatism during the 1950s swept back towards a hip liberalism and counter culture in the 1960s. With the movement came a gradual relaxation in attitudes towards drugs. Many Americans became more tolerant of recreational drug use, and a proliferation of psychoactive substances appeared on the streets.

Individuals such as Harvard professor Timothy Leary led the way in the early 1960s, rejecting America's traditional culture in lieu of self-discovery and altered states of consciousness. "My advice to myself and to everybody else, particularly young people," Leary offered, "is to turn on, tune in, and drop out."[1] Leary asserted that LSD, d-lysergic acid diethylamide, and its mind-expanding trips offered personal fulfillment and a panacea for alcoholism, war, violence, and other ills. Believing in "better living through chemistry," some Americans experimented with LSD impregnated in blotter paper, sugar cubes, and animal crackers. LSD was a legal drug until the mid-1960s when state and federal regulations prohibited its possession, manufacture, importation, and sale. As the Eighteenth Amendment had done to the cost of alcohol, these laws raised acid's street prices and made illicit LSD manufacture highly profitable for clandestine laboratories. LSD's popularity peaked about 1971 when an estimated five million Americans had used the drug.

■ *A poster by artist Greg Irons in 1967 is typical of the psychedelic art created during the late sixties and seventies. Many, designed specifically to advertise rock music groups, featured bright, psychedelic or dayglo colors that fluoresced under black light. Swirling text simulated the visual distortion a user might experience under the influence of LSD. Like the lyrics of rock music, many posters made sly—or unabashed—references to drug use. Lewis Carroll's* Alice in Wonderland *gained a new following among users who delighted in Alice's adventures with magic mushrooms and hookah-smoking caterpillars. Here Alice's tea party suggests the old slang for marijuana.*

if you TOOK LSD

you'd be THERE by NOW

■ *This bumper sticker from the mid-1970s reflects the more tolerant and humorous way many Americans regarded the use of hallucinogens and other drugs. Swiss chemist Albert Hoffman had accidentally discovered the potent psychoactive properties of LSD in 1943. He noted that after ingesting the drug, "I had to leave my work in the laboratory and go home because I felt strangely restless and dizzy. Once there, I lay down and sank into a not unpleasant delirium which was marked by an extreme degree of fantasy. In a sort of trance with closed eyes . . . fantastic visions of extraordinary vividness accompanied by a kaleidoscope of intense coloration continuously swirled around me."*

Although illicit LSD was still available, LSD-like drugs such as STP, MDA, and PCP came into use, sometimes fraudulently sold as LSD. Some people initially called PCP (phencyclidine) Angel Dust or the Peace Pill, believing that it broke down inhibitions and hostilities. Researchers had developed PCP as a surgical anesthetic in 1959, but negative side effects caused doctors to discontinue its use except in veterinary practice. Small doses produce pleasurable effects of relaxation and a floating sensation; large doses can result in hallucinations, bizarre, violent behavior, and insensitivity to pain. Illicit labs continued to produce PCP, but its reputation as an unpredictable substance reduced its popularity.

MDMA (3,4 Methylenedioxymethamphetamine) resurfaced from the past as Ecstasy. First developed in 1914 as an appetite suppressant, some doctors used MDMA in the 1970s as an emotive psychotherapy aid. It soon gained immense popular appeal as a legal recreational drug sold in bars. MDMA enhanced an individual's mood, sense of touch, and endurance. As one user recounted, "Ecstasy makes you what everyone wants to be. Self-assured, loving, friendly. It's the hug drug."[2] Opponents, however, claimed that a quantity only two or three times larger than the average street dose can cause brain damage. In 1985, the federal government reclassified the drug, and it became illegal.

Plant hallucinogens, including mescaline, morning glory seeds, nutmeg, peyote, and psilocybin provided organic highs for experimenting flower children of the sixties, but the drug of preference for many Americans from the late 1960s to the present was and remains marijuana.

For many Americans in the 1960s and early 1970s, marijuana represented a rejection both of the establishment responsible for the Vietnam War and of the conservative, traditional values of the 1950s. Rejecting the cocktails of their parents' generation, young Americans turned to marijuana, which they claimed pacified the user in contrast to the aggressive effects alcohol often exerted on the drinker. Approximately three hundred thousand concert goers at the 1969 Woodstock, New York, rock festival attributed the crowd's overall placid behavior—despite the lack of food and adequate facilities and despite an abundance of rain and mud—to its copious use of marijuana.

Just as some Americans of the 1870s found the lure of Eastern culture and hashish smoking irresistible, some modern marijuana users, intrigued with Eastern mysticism, saw marijuana as a way to help achieve inner peace and enlightenment. Perhaps the majority of users, however, simply perceived marijuana to be a harmless and natural alternative to alcohol. Troops stationed in Vietnam used marijuana so frequently that in 1968 the United States military launched an antimarijuana campaign. As historian H. Wayne Morgan commented,

The Army's heavy-handed crackdown on marijuana use seemed to turn many soldiers to heroin, which was easily procured and often cheap. By the spring of 1971, the press began to report a major heroin problem in Vietnam.[3]

The trauma of combat, death, and all the other stressful conditions inherent in war, including boredom, provoked some soldiers to use heroin. One Vietnam vet recalled, "I started in Vietnam. I was scared. I had got shot. It was a bullet straight through the thigh. The medics gave me a shot of morphine and they got me high and all of a sudden I forgot I got shot and I wasn't scared." After that experience, the soldier began injecting heroin before missions to overcome his fear of battle. ". . . each time we went in the jungle to a fire fight, I wanted the same feeling from my life."[4]

Conditions in the asphalt jungles of America's

■ A 1968 poster served as a wry commentary on the wide use of marijuana, or tea, by U. S. servicemen stationed in Vietnam. The phrase "flavor-seal lid" referred to the street term for one ounce of marijuana. Acapulco Gold, a variety of Mexican grown marijuana was popular, as was Panama Red and other varieties. This poster was published the same year that the U. S. army began its antimarijuana campaign, arresting one thousand servicemen in one week for possession of the drug. The following year a civilian antimarijuana campaign, Operation Intercept, was staged along the Mexican border.

Artist Angel Allende painted a modern day pieta scene in 1973. Set in the ghettos of East Harlem, New York, a mother mourns her dead son; the instrument of death, a hypodermic needle presumably containing heroin, lies close by. The painting laments the increased use of heroin by minorities living in the inner city during the 1970s. It also illustrates one of the dangers of heroin use. The difference between an effective dose of heroin and a lethal dose is relatively narrow, complicated by the fact that many users develop tolerance to the drug, thus requiring larger amounts to get high. Alcohol and barbiturates used in conjunction with heroin compound the risk of death. Adulterants, such as strychnine—present in many illicit drugs—may poison unsuspecting users. Courtesy, Museum of the City of New York, gift of Mr. and Mrs. Robert Wallace Gilmore.

inner cities were stressful too. Overcome by a sense of futility, some coped with poverty, unemployment, crime, and discrimination by using heroin. Contrary to the stereotyped image of the junkie whose entire day revolved around drug use, many users maintained a degree of control over their habit by using relatively small amounts. By 1970, approximately five hundred thousand Americans used heroin; about two hundred and fifty thousand of them lived in New York City.[5]

From the 1960s to the present, some teenagers conducted their own drug experiments by inhaling fumes from ordinary household products, such as glue, paints, solvents, cleaners, and pressurized dessert toppings. They often contained volatile or gaseous substances which produced an intoxication similar to drunkenness or hallucinations. Depending on the agent they inhaled, adventurous kids experienced side effects ranging from mild throat irritation to irreversible liver damage and death. Unfortunately, media coverage of glue sniffing episodes tended to encourage rather than discourage the practice.

Amphetamines, synthetic stimulants developed during the 1930s, also became popular among America's youth during the 1960s. In the Second World War, American, British, and Japanese pilots countered fatigue and depression with amphetamines. After the war, doctors continued prescribing oral doses of the drug for asthma, depression, hyperactivity, and weight reduction. A few physicians treated heroin addiction with intravenous injections of amphetamines. In 1962, some San Francisco doctors and pharmacies illegally sold injectable amphetamines, such as methedrine or speed. After injecting the drug, a user usually experienced intense euphoria and feelings of stamina before crashing when the drug wore off. Individuals injecting amphetamines quickly developed tolerance, the need for larger and larger doses to achieve the initial reaction, and often psychotic behaviors so bizarre that dependent users were labeled speed freaks. In 1965, poet Allen Ginsberg condemned the drug:

■ *As cheap cocaine flooded American cities and suburbs in the 1980s, head shops, once a source for marijuana paraphenalia, sold goods that some patrons might use in the consumption of cocaine. A Rochester, New York, head shop offered these items for sale in 1991. They include, clockwise from the top, a snuff inhaler, a plastic coke card, a gold plated set at center composed of a spoon, nasal straw, razor blade, and mirror, all available with monogramming. Users cut any large particles of cocaine on the mirror with the blade and shape the drug into thin lines before inhaling them. The gold plating prevents the acid in cocaine hydrochloride from rusting the equipment. Prefolded papers make neat and efficient packets for storing cocaine. The necklace at top left doubles as a cocaine spoon.*

■ *Crack users turn almost any object—a soft drink can or a fifty-cent test tube—into a pipe for inhaling crack. Dealers created the crack market around 1983, after a glut of cocaine dropped the price of that drug. Dealers withdrew cocaine and offered only crack, knowing that their customers would return again and again. By 1984, Colombian smugglers brought quantities of crack into Los Angeles, where members of the Crips and the Bloods gangs distributed it, running three crack houses that made $6,000 a day. Meanwhile, other dealers, the Jamaican Shower or posse, drew fifty-four hundred members in more than a dozen cities, including New York; Miami; Rochester, New York; Washington, D. C.; Detroit; and Toronto. The posse took its name from the violence that became their trademark: they showered opponents in blood.*

Let's issue a general declaration to all the underground community, *contra speedamos ex cathedra.* Speed is antisocial, paranoid making, it's a drag, bad for your body, bad for your mind, generally speaking, in the long run uncreative and it's a plague in the whole dope industry. All the nice gentle dope fiends are getting screwed up by the real horror monster Frankenstein speed freaks who are going around stealing and bad mouthing everybody.[6]

The Food and Drug Administration launched a stringent antispeed campaign and restricted distribution of amphetamines. Inadvertently, the ban served to popularize the drug, and illicit speed labs sprang up. The black market also diverted supplies of legally produced amphetamines.

As law enforcement agencies cracked down on the amphetamine trade, another stimulant, cocaine, reappeared around 1970. Called the champagne of drugs, the stimulant became the drug of choice in more affluent circles of movie and rock stars and other celebrities. In the 1970s, Studio 54, New York's chic and trendy discotheque, regaled customers each night by lowering a large paper moon that sprinkled white powder over the dance floor while a man in the moon spooned cocaine. Movie director and author Peter Bogdanovich summarized cocaine's appeal:

Cocaine gives an icy-cold high that freezes your heart and makes you believe you are all-powerful, invincible, and righteously correct in all of your appetites and impulses. . . . If grass is the drug of peace, cocaine is the drug of war.[7]

In 1982, a cocaine glut dropped prices, spreading its appeal among many middle class Americans. But soon the press reported cocaine related illnesses and deaths, such as that of comedian John Belushi in 1982, causing cocaine's popularity to dip slightly.

■ *Reinforced with sheet metal, angle irons, and eight bolts, this door, confiscated from a Rochester, New York, gate house, once stood between drug dealers and their customers and the police. The dealers sell their drugs through a small slot cut into an exterior wall. Most dealers have an escape route; fortified doors and windows, such as this one, are designed to detain police as the dealers flee. In many American cities, drug dealers have devastated neighborhoods, moving into apartments and houses in low-rent areas which all too often become the scene of theft, assault, and homicide, in addition to drug trafficking.* Courtesy, Rochester Police Department.

■ *Like their nineteenth-century counterparts, contemporary newspapers report hair-raising accounts of drug use. Ron Tarver of* The Philadelphia Inquirer *photographed this gate house or drug house in 1991. Patrons pay an admission charge of a dollar or so; inside they find drugs, clean bottle caps for cooking heroin, and bleach for disinfecting needles. Because the Philadelphia jails are so overcrowded, most street dealers cannot be imprisoned while awaiting trial, unless they are caught with more than fifty pounds of marijuana, fifty grams of heroin or cocaine, or ten grams of crack. The lure of profits guarantees an endless stream of dealers to replace those who do wind up in jail.* Courtesy, Ron Tarver, *The Philadelphia Inquirer.*

■ *These glycine bags bear the trademark "D.O.A." for Death on Arrival, one brand of heroin sold in Rochester, New York, in 1991. Drug dealers often use glycine bags to package heroin. Like good advertisers everywhere, dealers create catchy names for their wares. Far from turning customers off, such names make users all the more eager to buy—the deadlier the name, the purer and more potent the product appears.* Courtesy, Rochester Police Department.

Designer drugs took up the slack. Chemists developed designer drugs or analogs by slightly altering the chemical structure of a parent drug. The analogs, at least until the federal government outlawed them, were thus not illegal. Another new drug emerged as drug dealers and users experimented with cocaine. They combined the drug with baking soda, soaked it in water, then applied heat which caused the substance to give off a crackling sound, hence the drug's street name, crack. The method produced a hard cake that dealers cut into rocks or chunks and sold for three to ten dollars each. Drug dealers, aided by the Los Angeles gangs, the Crips and the Bloods, flooded many cities with cheap crack, "the poor man's cocaine," in the mid-1980s. When smoked, crack reaches the brain in about eight seconds, causing an intense but short-lived high—which many users are anxious to repeat. Crack, thus, is highly addictive, guaranteeing dealers a steady clientele.

Surgeons briefly used another designer drug, fentanyl, a synthetic opiate many times stronger than morphine, to anesthetize patients but discarded the drug after observing negative side effects. Dealers, working in illicit labs, sometimes blended fentanyl with other drugs despite the possibly lethal consequences. In February 1991, a batch of heroin mixed with fentanyl, marketed as Tango and Cash, killed seventeen people and hospitalized two hundred others in one weekend.

Although illicit drugs received the lion's share of media attention, the use and misuse of certain prescription drugs, particularly barbiturates and minor tranquilizers escalated during the 1960s and seventies. Barbiturates entered medical practice in 1903 under the name of Veronal; phenobarbital followed in 1912. These and many other barbiturates induced sleep and relieved anxiety. By the 1930s, "an estimated *billion* grains were being taken each year in the United States alone."[8] In many respects, barbiturates resembled alcohol: users could become intoxicated, or high; and, if taken steadily, barbiturates produced dependence and withdrawal symptoms. In 1949, the Food and Drug Administration portrayed barbiturates as thrill pills that induced intoxication. Although there were reports of earlier misuse, the warnings lured many Americans into experimenting with barbiturates, often together with alcohol—a potentially deadly combination. A former addict recalled his dependence on barbiturates in the late 1950s and early 1960s:

A well-meaning friend introduced me to the joys of Seconal. He called them "saggies," there's a hundred names for these things. . . . If you take it before going in to a party and your intention is to get high, you'll get high. One Seconal gave place to two, then four. Then I began to experiment, as people will. The Seconal gave way to Tuinal, then Placidyl, and then the whole army of these barbiturates. [I] . . . had a little case made for me with twelve vials, six on each side. I called it my "how-do-I-want-to-feel-today kit." It was very funny in those days: I'd open it and people would get hysterical, because there was every color in the rainbow in those glass vials. It was a laugh. . . . Sharing the pills with them made me more socially acceptable in their group.[9]

Drug companies developed new less potent antianxiety drugs—classified as minor tranquilizers—which were similar to barbiturates in many ways. Miltown and Equanil entered the market in the 1950s, followed by Librium around 1960 and later by Valium. Shrewdly promoted as a simple, modern treatment for stress caused by everything from job changes to menopause and aging, Valium was the number one prescription drug during the 1960s.

"I never thought of Valium as a real drug," commented one young woman who became dependent upon Valium,

I put it on the same level drug-wise with aspirin. *Everybody* takes Valium, I thought—it's the number-one prescription drug in the country. . . . I have friends who won't walk out of the door without their little vial of Valium.[10]

Society responded to the rise in drug use through medical and legal channels, which generally reflected a more lenient approach towards some drugs. Under President John F. Kennedy's administration, more federal monies funded mental health centers where addiction was viewed as a health issue. Therapeutic communities or "TC's" emerged in the 1960s, such as Daytop, Odyssey House, and Phoenix House, initially influenced by Synanon, a therapeutic community founded in 1958. These centers offered long-term care and rehabilitation to help an individual restructure his or her life. Staffed by former drug users, therapeutic communities endeavor to instill self-discipline and self-esteem. Their regimes are strict and unbending. Unfortunately, Synanon gained a controversial reputation by the late 1970s when both staff and residents reported abusive treatment by the institution's administration.

In 1962, the same year that Federal Bureau of Narcotics head Harry Anslinger retired, the U. S. Supreme Court formally ruled that addiction was a disease and not a crime per se. The Court's ruling paved the way for methadone maintenance programs for heroin addicts, a plan that substituted methadone, a synthetic opiate developed during the Second World War, for heroin. Two doctors, Vincent Dole and Marie Nyswander, who pioneered the program, theorized that heroin caused perma-

NO EASY ANSWERS

Researchers, physicians, psychiatrists and other health care professionals continue to study the causes of chemical dependency in an effort to discover more successful treatments. Guiding those treatments are several theories concerning the nature of chemical dependence. Some physicians subscribe to the subculture theory, which asserts that people use drugs to feel like they belong. These people learn to use drugs from individuals they like or admire. Conversely, people who do not use drugs tend not to associate with those who do. The setting in which people use drugs may be a key factor, demonstrated by the fact that most Vietnam veterans who had used heroin overseas discontinued using the drug once removed from the war-torn environment.

Other counselors suggest that there is an addictive personality type who is likely to become drug dependent. Generally, this person is unable to cope with the daily stresses around him or her, has low self-esteem, but is adventuresome, nonconforming, and unconventional.

Some researchers believe that individuals may inherit genes that predispose them towards alcohol and other drug dependency. "Faulty" genes produce "faulty" enzymes that disrupt the normal metabolism of alcohol. This theory could explain why alcoholism often seems to run in families.

Another theory asserts that some drugs upset the brain's normal chemistry. Constant use of drugs such as cocaine, opiates, and alcohol may create a chemical imbalance producing withdrawal symptoms and a physical craving for drugs. In some cases, drugs may permanently damage nerve cells, resulting in radical alterations in the body and mind.

By the mid-1980s, some psychiatrists adapted a broader view of addiction, using it to include compulsive activities such as gambling, shopping, overeating, and undereating. "Addictions are characterized by a compulsion, a loss of control, and continuing despite harmful consequences," wrote psychiatrist Harvey Milkman. "By that definition, one can be addicted to a behavior, just as to drugs." Other experts disagree, arguing that the treatment of a biological substance dependency may differ greatly from a behavioral disorder.

Until fairly recently, scientists defined chemical dependency or addiction more circumspectly. Physical dependency was defined by the presence of withdrawal symptoms when a substance was withheld and of tolerance, the need to increase dosages to achieve the same initial reaction. Psychological addiction was characterized by a compulsive need to use the drug but not necessarily by withdrawal and tolerance. The American Psychiatric Association believes a substance dependency or addiction exists if three or more of the following statements are true:

- The substance is taken in larger amounts or over a longer period than the person intended.

- There is a persistent desire or unsuccessful attempt to stop.

- The person spends a great deal of time trying to get the substance, e.g. robberies to raise the money, taking the drug, or recovering from its effects.

- Using the substance disrupts important social obligations or work activities.

- The person continues to use the substance despite knowing that it is causing problems, e.g. drinking even though it makes an ulcer worse.

- There is marked tolerance. The person needs markedly increased amounts of the substance to become intoxicated or has a marked reduction of the desired effect if using the same amount.

- There are withdrawal symptoms.

- The substance is taken to avoid withdrawal symptoms.

In 1935, stockbroker William Wilson and Dr. Robert Smith, both alcoholics, pledged to help each other stay sober. The support they each gave and their Twelve Steps recovery plan brought success—which they shared with other alcoholics. In 1939, Alcoholics Anonymous formed, offering hope and fellowship to many. The success rate was such that many treatment centers adopted the Twelve Steps for those recovering from other chemical dependencies and emotional problems.

The 12 Steps of A.A.

1. We admitted we were powerless over alcohol—that our lives had become unmanageable. 2. Came to believe that a Power greater than ourselves could restore us to sanity. 3. Made a decision to turn our will and our lives over to the care of God *as we understood Him*. 4. Made a searching and fearless moral inventory of ourselves. 5. Admitted to God, to ourselves, and to another human being the exact nature of our wrongs. 6. Were entirely ready to have God remove all these defects of character. 7. Humbly asked Him to remove our shortcomings. 8. Made a list of all persons we had harmed, and became willing to make amends to them all. 9. Made direct amends to such people wherever possible, except when to do so would injure them or others. 10. Continued to take personal inventory and when we were wrong promptly admitted it. 11. Sought through prayer and meditation to improve our conscious contact with God *as we understood Him*, praying only for knowledge of His will for us and the power to carry that out. 12. Having had a spiritual awakening as the result of these steps, we tried to carry this message to alcoholics, and to practice these principles in all our affairs.

Steps and Traditions copyright © by A.A. World Services, Inc.

NO SMOKING

■ *Photographer Alfred Gescheidt created this ghostly image to convey the dangers of smoking for a poster published around 1975. Aversion techniques in drug education are not unwarranted considering that, according to the American Cancer Society, approximately 320,000 Americans die prematurely because of coronary heart disease, cancer, and other lung diseases caused by smoking. As Surgeon General C. Everett Koop reported in 1980, cigarette smoking is the "single most important preventable cause of death and disease."*

nent biochemical changes resulting in an addict's dependency, thus, the addict required maintenance. Although methadone was equally addicting, Dole and Nyswander argued that the drug, safely and legally administered, offered addicts a chance for a stable, crime free life.

Many patients had—and still have—mixed feelings about methadone. It eliminated the risks of obtaining illegal, and sometimes adulterated, drugs and the danger of using contaminated needles, but methadone presented its own set of health problems and side effects. Critics charged that methadone maintenance was another form of social control aimed at minorities who are numbered among the addicts. Patients on methadone have registered the drug's advantages and disadvantages. One commented,

Methadone's a crutch, in a way. You feel safe. I've said so many times, "I wonder what I'd be doing if there wasn't any methadone program?" I wondered if I'd still be alive. Because, without methadone, it would have been heroin, or cocaine, or something else.

Another argued,

I think that they're not being entirely fair to the patient, in that they don't give him warning that he's

■ *This collection of confiscated pipes, bongs, and roach clips used for smoking marijuana between 1980–1990 reveals the ingenuity and aesthetics of some of their makers. Plumbing supplies and everyday items such as pens, bottles, and car parts, have been used to create smoking paraphernalia. For the less inventive, head shops offer a wide array of "unusual smoking accessories." Although marijuana use has declined because of its high prices, it is the most commonly used recreational drug after caffeine, tobacco, and alcohol.*
Courtesy, Fitz Hugh Ludlow Memorial Library, David Monk, and Gary Metz.

Decriminalize Marijuana

SIGN PETITION HERE

FOR MORE INFORMATION CONTACT:

■ *A petition, printed in patriotic red, white, and blue ink in the early 1970s, reflected the changing attitudes about marijuana. Some Americans believed—and continue to believe—that states should license marijuana sales just as they do alcohol sales. Groups such as NORML (National Organization for the Reform of Marijuana Laws) and HEMP organized to campaign for the legalization of marijuana. Besides endorsing marijuana's recreational use, these and other associations encourage research into the medical and commercial applications of hemp or cannabis—of the latter, particularly in the production of paper, cloth, and fuel.* Courtesy, Fitz Hugh Ludlow Memorial Library.

going into treatment that lasts a lifetime. . . . Methadone is much better than . . . Demerol though. It's better for the very simple reason that I lead a normal life. I don't have to scheme to get drugs. I no longer need a drug so long as I drink my medication every morning with a little bit of orange juice. . . . I'm on a leash. I'm retired, I have no financial worries, . . . and I plan to travel. Say I wanted to go to Kansas City or Indianapolis, or Baton Rouge. I would first have to get an OK from my clinic doctor. That would be readily given, but he is restricted to giving me medication for only a certain number of days. I can't go abroad. That's what I meant by the leash. It's always there.[11]

While Dole and Nyswander were researching the effects of methadone, other scientists and doctors were studying the effects of a much more familiar substance, nicotine. In 1964, after a seven-year study, the U.S. Surgeon General issued a warning that smoking was a health hazard. The news was unwelcome, not only to smokers who spent approximately $7 billion a year for cigarettes, but to the tobacco industry, to its thirty-four thousand workers and its advertising agencies, and to state governments who collected substantial revenues on tobacco sales.[12] The following year, cigarette sales actually rose by 716 billion cigarettes. Meanwhile in Congress, powerful tobacco lobbies blocked bills designed to curtail tobacco advertising and to require warning labels on product packaging that disclosed tobacco's health risks. Pressure exerted by the American Cancer Society, the United States Public Health Service, other agencies, and the increased numbers of Americans dying from lung cancer, emphysema, and heart disease eventually resulted in rulings that demanded health warnings in all cigarette advertising (1969) and a ban on television advertisements (1972).

The news media, however, focused more intently on America's consumption of illicit drugs, which increasingly challenged enforcement agencies. Marijuana arrests rocketed from 18,000 in 1965 to 188,000 in 1970.[13] Federal agencies launched Operation Intercept, a drive to confiscate drugs, particularly marijuana, smuggled into the United States from Mexico. But despite such measures, more and more Americans persisted in using the drug; by 1979, an estimated fifty million Americans had tried the drug at least once.[14] The hardy plant was easy to grow in the home under grow-lights or in the wild. California marijuana growers organized a guild to support legal action protecting domestic cultivation while magazines and journals provided them with farming tips and information on different varieties of marijuana such as Sierra Sinemillia. The Emerald Triangle, a ten-thousand-square-mile stretch of national forest in Northern California, became a large center of production. Law enforcement agencies used helicopters for surveillance.

But as more and more citizens used marijuana without disastrous effects, opinions mellowed and many Americans began making distinctions between a soft drug like marijuana and hard drugs like heroin. In 1970, a group called NORML, or the National Organization for the Reform of Marijuana Laws, formed to promote legalization of the drug. In the same year, the Comprehensive Drug Abuse and Control Act of 1970 abolished mandatory, minimum jail terms and lessened the penalties for simple possession of marijuana. This act also reorganized legislation of controlled substances. It established five schedules for the classification of drugs according to their potential for dependency and medical use. In 1972-1973, a thirteen member team chosen by President Richard M. Nixon and the Speaker of the House formed a Commission on Marijuana and Drug Abuse which recommended that marijuana possession be decriminalized.

Whereas many Americans were willing to take a more lenient stance on marijuana use, heroin scared nearly everyone, particularly after the press reported that approximately 25 percent of Vietnam veterans allegedly used the substance. In response to heroin's growing appeal, President Richard M. Nixon declared an official "war on drugs" in 1971. Under Nixon's administration, Turkey, the main supplier of heroin, agreed to reduce its poppy cultivation in return for U. S. financial aid. As historian David Musto has observed, however, the "slack in supply was taken up by Mexican production and other suppliers from Southeast Asia's Golden Triangle, Afghanistan, Pakistan, and so on."[15] Nixon also authorized creation of the Drug Enforcement Agency, the National Institute on Drug Abuse, and the Special Action Office for Drug Abuse Prevention which in turn fostered many treatment and research programs. As a result, scientists made important discoveries regarding how opiates affect the brain and other organs. Scientists Candace Pert and Solomon Snyder, for example, isolated specific sites or receptors on nerve cells with which opioid drugs interacted. This led to the discovery of endorphins, the "body's own morphine," a naturally occurring protein that resembles opioids. These and other breakthroughs helped scientists and doctors to understand better the physical mechanisms of opioid dependency.

The war on drugs eased during the administration of President Gerald R. Ford. The White House candidly admitted "Total elimination of drug abuse is unlikely," adding, "all drugs are not equally dangerous, and all drug use is not equally destructive."[16] The official stance was to eradicate the most dangerous drugs, which were recognized to be heroin, amphetamines, and mixed barbiturates, but not necessarily cocaine or marijuana. In fact, opinions had shifted so dramatically, that in 1977, President Jimmy Carter's administration, under the advisement of drug expert Dr. Peter Bourne, confidently advocated legalizing the possession of less than one ounce of marijuana. As for cocaine, Dr. Bourne remarked:

Cocaine . . . is probably the most benign of illicit drugs currently in widespread use. At least as strong a case could be made for legalizing it as for legalizing marijuana. Short acting—about 15 minutes—not physically addicting, and acutely pleasurable, cocaine has found increasing favor at all socioeconomic levels in the last year.[17]

■ *Like the temperance movement of the 1830s and 1870s, the Just Say No campaign turned its attention to the young, hoping that an informed younger generation would better resist the temptations of drug use. Clockwise from top center is a child's 1992 pledge card, a weekly reader distributed through the New York State public school system, and two give-aways from Rochester area firms, a Just Say No bag and a Hugs Not Drugs button.*

But as the Carter administration considered the legalization issue, the pendulum was already beginning its backward swing. In the late 1970s, concerned parents formed groups, such as the National Federation of Parents for Drug-Free Youth, to voice their opposition to drug use, including marijuana. The movement gained further momentum from the conservative administration of President Ronald Reagan, the widespread use of cocaine, and the cocaine related deaths of celebrities such as comedian John Belushi in 1982 and rising basketball star Len Bias in 1986. No longer viewed simply as a "benign" substance, cocaine acquired a menacing reputation. As reports that a crack cocaine epidemic was sweeping the inner cities, increasing crime, destroying neighborhoods, triggering gang violence, and leaving a generation of "crack-addicted babies," public opinion recoiled from drug use. Then in 1986, the American Association of Advertising Agencies formed the Partnership for a Drug-free America, recruiting services and donations from the media and advertisers. The organization saturated national television with 293 antidrug commercials.

On August 4, 1986, President Reagan declared a second war on drugs. Later that month, he and wife Nancy Reagan appeared together on national television, launching the Just Say No campaign. "You have the responsibility to be intolerant of drug use anywhere, anytime, by anybody," stated Nancy Reagan. "You have the responsibility of forcing the issue to the point of making others uncomfortable and yourself unpopular."[18] The Just Say No campaign focused public attention on drug use, drawing both its supporters and its critics who argued that the simplistic approach had little hope of working in the grim environment of the inner city. Nevertheless, as a result of the emphasis on prevention, most public school systems mandated drug education curricula. Many businesses also introduced employee drug testing. In 1983, only 2 percent of the Fortune 500 companies tested employees; by 1992, 80 percent use these tests, setting off arguments between those who believe such tests are an invasion of privacy and those who contend that the benefits of drug testing outweigh the

rights of the individual.[19]

In 1986, President Reagan signed into law the Anti-Drug Abuse Act which appropriated nearly $4 billion for drug control, primarily for law enforcement. The war, however, was not over. On September 5, 1989, President George Bush declared yet another war on drugs, "the gravest domestic threat," in his first televised speech as president. With drug czar William Bennett in command of a militaristic crusade, approximately 70 percent of the $10 billion budget funded law enforcement and 30 percent funded treatment and prevention. Bennett favored tougher sentencing and more vigorous law enforcement, which burdened an already overtaxed judicial and prison system. According to William Lokyer, chairman of the Senate Judiciary Committee in the California legislature, Bennett's sentencing proposals alone "would add $5 billion to a state budget already $3.6 billion in the red."[20] In 1990, Bennett announced that illicit drug use had declined, although his critics observed that while casual drug use in the suburbs had decreased, the rate of drug use in urban areas remained fairly constant.

Drug use in America is in part due to the global and political nature of the drug trade that floods the country with its products. Production of illicit substances is a multibillion dollar, international industry with sophisticated distribution networks. In many Third World countries, such as Colombia, Bolivia, and Mexico, revenues from illicit drugs provide desperately needed income. A Colombian laborer earns $3.50 a day picking coffee but makes $25.00 picking coca leaves.[21] Drug dealers know a ready market awaits them in the United States.

DISCRIMINATION

POSSIBILITY OF A DOUBT.

Dugan. — Iverything do be an th' square in this place, Brady!
Brady (who has just realized that he is being played) — Oh! Oi don't know. This is th' fifth round Oi 've paid for!

■ *Nineteenth-century newspapers and magazines, like* Puck, *often depicted Irish Americans in a negative light. Ridiculing their accents, traditions, and culture, the cartoons instilled in some Americans the unjustified beliefs that Irish Americans drank too much and were difficult to train for new jobs. This imagery was partly responsible for keeping many Irish immigrants locked in the impoverished underclass. Frustrated by unemployment, low wages, and discrimination, some Irish Americans solaced themselves with drink. The rowdy were incarcerated; the many Irish arrests led some to call a police patrol wagon a "paddy wagon."*

Discrimination and drugs have gone hand in hand throughout American history. Americans' fears of ethnic groups have led to distorted perceptions about drug use within particular communities.

In the eighteenth and nineteenth centuries, some white Americans used alcohol to control native Americans and African Americans, withholding it to segregate, dispensing it to exploit. Many Americans resented the large waves of poor Irish Catholics immigrating to America in the 1840s. With them came whiskey-drinking traditions—just when many middle class Americans gave up alcohol. The press reinforced stereotypes by portraying Irish workers as stupid and habitually drunk. The incarceration rate for Irish Americans was disproportionately high; as one immigrant complained, "The constable shushed native boisterousness; they arrested the boisterous Irish. They helped home a native drunk; the Irish drunk landed behind bars."[1]

In contrast, skilled Protestant German immigrants more easily blended into American society. But they also faced discrimination because of cultural differences—including beer drinking. Some Americans worried that the urban German beer garden and saloon (with its back room for meetings) would spawn labor unions and radical political parties. In 1882, Ohio's Governor Charles Foster campaigned against Sunday openings of beer gardens in Cincinnati, characterizing "Dutch" brewers as "Sabbath breakers, criminals, and free thinkers." The Ohio State Brewers' and Maltsters' Association replied, "We feel justified in believing that your original plan...was to attack Germans."[2]

By the 1870s, many Americans on both coasts felt threatened by Chinese immigrants. Nativists scorned differences in Chinese language, dress, religion, and their recreational use of opium. Chinese neighborhood organizations called tongs increasingly controlled the opium trade and pros-

■ The Ohio Dry Association of Columbus, Ohio, printed this poster, "The Kaiser Chuckles," in 1917. By the twentieth century, many German Americans had assimilated into American society, but the First World War brought a backlash of suspicion and distrust that Prohibitionists used to their own advantage. In a wave of anti-German fervor, many Americans turned against individuals and breweries that had German-sounding names. The drys could not have been happier; they portrayed the drinking of lager as a German-inspired plot designed to divert food from America's war effort.

■ The large numbers of poor Chinese laborers who came to the United States disquieted some Americans who blamed these immigrants for the country's economic problems—and the increased use of opium among white Americans. Journals such as Harper's Weekly portrayed Chinese opium dealers luring white women first into drug use—and then into white slavery, convincing some Americans that the Chinese were subversive and dangerous members of society.

The Kaiser Chuckles
Every Bushel of Grain that is diverted from supplying American Soldiers with Bread; from supplying American Workmen with Bread, is helping the Kaiser's game.

If the Kaiser could *he would reach out his bloody hand and pat the man on the back* who is boosting his game here in Ohio by voting wet.

Ohio has no grain to waste on beer or booze—now or ever—Ohio needs every ounce of grain for her soldiers and workers and for a hungry and starving world.

Vote Yes on Prohibition Nov. 5th.

Arrest for Burglary
Two Counts

MANUEL ONITIVERAS, a
MANUEL CHAVEZ;

A Mexican;
Age about 30 years,
height about 6 feet,
weight about 150 lbs
slender build,
smooth shaven,
medium sallow com-
plexion, black hair,
dark eyes,
a marihuana fiend.

Has two suits, one a grey and oth
dark; has two hats, one light colo
other dark.
I hold Felony Warrants. Notify

O. W. B.
Supt. B. of I.

W. A. SHAY, Sh

Or A. A. BURCHAM, Chief of Police, San Bernardino

■ *For some Americans, marijuana provided a tool for their discrim-*
inating against Mexican immigrants during the 1930s and 1940s.
Just as many Southerners believed that cocaine would lead to civil
unrest among African Americans, some Westerners claimed that mar-
ijuana made Mexicans wild, violent, and criminal, as this poster
indicates. Many Americans campaigned to outlaw medical uses of
cannabis and lobbied for laws that strictly controlled its sale. They
hoped that such laws would persuade some Mexicans to return to
their native land. Courtesy, Michael Aldrich, Aldrich Archives.

titution. As the tongs' reputation for lawlessness grew, nativists pounced on their use of opium. One Oregon district court judge reflected, "Opium smoking is not our vice, and therefore it may be that this legislation proceeds more from a desire to vex and annoy the Heathen Chinese in this respect than to protect the people from the evil habit."[3]

In the twentieth century, African Americans and Hispanic Americans have often borne the brunt of discrimination. Whereas the rates for drug use are similar for both whites and blacks, African Americans more frequently face imprisonment. Twenty-five percent of young black males are either in prison or have been in prison. Treatment programs are more readily accessible to white patients than to blacks or Hispanics. Historian David Musto commented on the tendency to scapegoat drugs for many social ills. "It allows us to ascribe all the profound social problems of the inner city to one thing—drugs. . . . That lets the rest of us off the hook, free to ignore the deeper problems of unemployment and lack of education."[4]

NOTES

1. Richard Stivers, *A Hair of the Dog: Irish Drinking and American Stereotype*, (University Park: The Pennsylvania State Press, 1976), 141.

2. Ohio State Brewers' and Maltsters' Association, *An Open Letter to His Excellency, Gov. Foster* (Cincinnati: The Ohio State Brewers' and Maltsters' Association, 8 September, 1882) n.p., The Strong Museum Library, Rochester, New York.

3. John Helmer, *Drugs and Minority Suppression,* (New York: Seabury Press, 1975), 39–40.

4. David Musto, *Time* (3 December 1990), 47.

■ *Out of work and out of hope, these heroin addicts shoot up in The Graveyard, a ghetto narcotics den in Washington, D. C. Much of their time revolves around procuring and using drugs—euphemistically called "taking care of business." While the drug trade among minorities may be more visible, conducted in the open on city streets, most studies indicate that drug use for white, black, and Hispanic Americans is proportionally the same. But as historian David Musto has cautioned: "By pretending that most addicts are dark-skinned and destitute, middle-class Americans can avoid responsibility for confronting the reality of drug abuse among their own families and friends."* Courtesy, Tony O'Brian JB Pictures.

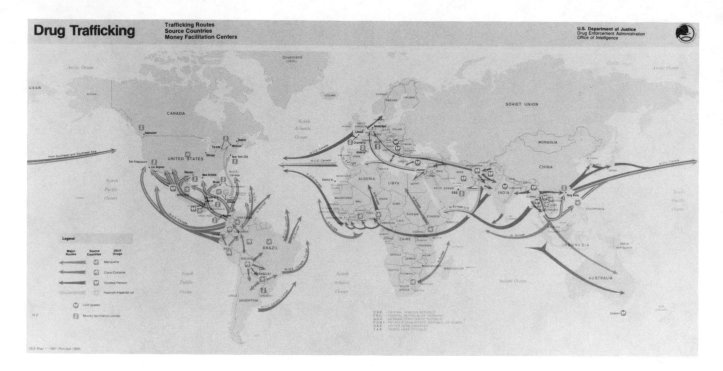

■ *This 1989 map charts the main trafficking routes, sources, and monetary centers of the international trade in marijuana, opiates, cocaine, and hashish. Although Peru and Bolivia grow much of the illicit coca, the Colombian Medellin and Cali cartels dominate cocaine production and distribution. When interviewed by* Time *(July 1, 1991), about the cocaine trade, Cali cartel leader and drug lord Gilberto Rodriquez commented, "Economics has a natural law: Supply is determined by the demand. When cocaine stops being consumed, when there is no demand for it . . . that will be the end of the business."*

America's war on drugs has stretched beyond the United States to foreign shores, provoking much dispute and derision. Critics, such as economics editor Jonathan Marshall, have observed:

U. S. drug programs abroad have sometimes served to overcome congressional reluctance to aid foreign security forces—many of which profit on the side from the drug trade—in their war against left wing guerrilla movements. This explains why so much of U. S. narcotics assistance is in the form of military aid, rather than as economic support for crop substitution.[22]

No less controversial was the Supreme Court's June 15, 1992, decision that the United States may kidnap suspected drug dealers from foreign countries for trial in the United States, even if the suspects are foreign nationals, even if their countries object, and even if extradition procedures are already specified by treaty.

In 1992, the federal government's spending on drug control approximated $12 billion. While advocates of government spending note a decline in casual drug use, others, such as Milton Friedman, the

Nobel laureate in economics, correlate the present homicide and prisoner rates with the war on drugs:

Granted that the whole . . . may not be attributable to the war on drugs. . . . Even if only half the effect is attributed to the war on drugs, 5,000 extra homicides a year and 45,000 extra prisoners is a high cost, and that price does not include the lives lost in Colombia, Peru, and elsewhere, or the lives lost through adulterated drugs in a black market, or the culture of violence, disrespect for the law, corruption of law enforcement officials and disregard of civil liberties unleashed by the war on drugs.[23]

The war on illicit drugs, however, is only part of the broader temperance movement that settled over the nation during the late 1980s and early 1990s. Alcohol and tobacco figure strongly in the new crusade.

Throughout the 1980s, alcohol consumption generally declined. Many states raised the legal age

■ *Police officers in Rochester, New York, display a few of the many weapons confiscated as evidence in drug-related crimes. They can collect up to a thousand guns during a three-month period. When no longer needed as evidence, the police destroy the weapon—but the holding room quickly refills. Police officers across the nation find themselves increasingly outgunned by drug dealers armed with sophisticated firearms, including military-type weapons such as the U. S.-made Commando Mark III semi-automatic machine gun, the AK–47 imported from Russia or China, and the Israeli .9mm Uze. Dealers, drawn to the trade by high profits, protect their turf from rival dealers and the police with these and other sophisticatd firearms. These weapons have an increased firepower, are more reliable than the cheap "Saturday night specials" common in the 1960s and 1970s, and range from an accessible $50 to $500. From top row, left to right: Maverick .12 gauge, pump shotgun; Commando Mark III, .45 caliber, semi-automatic rifle. Row 2, Hunter Arms, double-barrel sawed-off .12 gauge shotgun; Lone Star .22 caliber semi-automatic rifle; U. S. military M-I .30 caliber semi-automatic rifle. Row 3, Luger .9 mm semi-automatic rifle; M.K. Arms .9mm automatic rifle. Row 4, Smith and Wesson Python, .357 magnum revolver; Israeli Uze .9mm semi-automatic rifle.*

of drinking to twenty-one, and many Americans switched from distilled liquors to beverages with a lower alcohol content, such as beer, wine, and wine coolers. Organizations including Mothers Against Drunk Driving (MADD) and the Harvard Alcohol Project raised public awareness regarding the harmful effects of alcohol. Under pressure from these and other groups, numerous restaurants and bars ended their happy hours, which had encouraged copious drinking. While alcohol-related illnesses declined, however, the level of fatalities involving drunk driving has remained relatively high. According to the National Highway Safety Administration, of the 45,555 people who died in traffic accidents in the United States in 1989, 22,415 or 49.2 percent died in crashes involving alcohol use.[24]

Surgeon General Antonia Novello initiated a campaign against advertising strategies that target ethnic groups and underaged drinkers. High on her list was the Canandaigua Wine Company, maker of Cisco, a fortified wine packaged to look like soda, followed by the manufacturers of malt liquors such as PowerMaster, Midnight Dragon, and Turbo 1000, high alcohol products aimed at poor, urban, African American and Hispanic communities. While some members of the alcohol industry charge Novello with a neo-Prohibitionist agenda, the surgeon general has pointed to several undeniable facts. Teenaged binge drinking has increased in the last several years, and minorities suffer a disproportionately high rate of alcohol related illnesses.

Cirrhosis mortality is twice as common among black males as it is among white males nationally. . . . The rate of cancer of the esophagus among black males 35-

44 years old—a condition closely linked to alcohol consumption (and smoking)—is a staggering *ten times* that of their white counterparts.[25]

A fervent antismoking crusade accelerated in the 1980s under the leadership of Surgeon General C. Everett Koop. Ironically, tobacco, a legal substance subsidized by the federal government, is responsible for approximately 434,000 deaths a year whereas deaths related to cocaine and heroin overdose approximate 4,678. U. S. Health and Human Services Secretary Louis Sullivan has urged sports fans to boycott events, such as the Virginia Slims tennis tournament, sponsored by tobacco companies. Johns Hopkins University, Harvard, and the City University of New York decided to sell their stocks and bonds in companies with tobacco holdings, stating that ownership of such stocks is incompatible with the universities' missions to study and to treat cancer and other diseases. Increasingly, private business, such as the airline industry, have decided to ban or restrict smoking in keeping with stricter antismoking legislation.

As part of a national effort to reduce health problems caused by smoking, Surgeon General Novello has sharply criticized firms who aim advertisements of tobacco products at minorities, youth, the poor, and uneducated young women. Camel's Old Joe cigarette campaign, which uses cartoonlike camel characters that are especially appealing to young children, became one of the targets of Novello's wrath. Despite warnings and requests from the surgeon general, RJR, manufacturer of Camel cigarettes, not only refused to halt the advertising campaign, but intensified its promotion with free calendars and jackets bearing images of the offending quadrupeds and with advertising displays and fixtures in stores frequented by young adults. Opponents have replied across the nation with "Dump the Hump" parades and other protests. Patrick Reynolds, the grandson of the company's founder, criticizes present-day American tobacco trade which, faced with a declining domestic market, has steadily increased cigarette exports and advertising in Japan, China, Taiwan, and Eastern Europe. Confronting estimates that by 2025, about 7 million people in Third World countries will be dying of tobacco related diseases, the World Bank refused to finance tobacco growing, processing, and marketing.[26]

Another major health threat that has had an impact on modern drug use is AIDS, Acquired Immune Deficiency Syndrome. One of the greatest threats to intravenous drug users—and their sex partners and children—is the HIV virus that causes the fatal disease AIDS, spread by bodily fluids and infected hypodermic needles. Health workers estimate that nearly 50 percent of New York City's 250,000 IV drug users carry the virus, and that it is likely to spread into the general population.[27] Although the DEA and state legislatures have opposed clean needle exchange programs, New York Mayor David Dinkins and Washington, D. C. Mayor Sharon Pratt Kelley approved community based needle exchange programs in order to reduce infection rates.

The AIDS epidemic affects patterns of drug use in other ways. Because so many New York IV users are believed to be carrying the virus, many addicts now avoid the so-called shooting galleries where hypodermic needles are passed from one user to the next. As one New York heroin addict admit-

■ *This glazed paper and cloth jacket from China was part of a 1992 promotional campaign, given away "free" by convenience stores and gas stations when patrons purchased Camel cigarettes. Old Joe, the cigarette-smoking camel, appeared in 1988 to boost the sagging sales of RJR's Camel brand cigarettes. On May 16, 1992,* The Economist *quoted David Adleman, an analyst at Dean Witter Reynolds, who reported : "Before the campaign, the brand was in free fall. The turnaround has been miraculous." Sales among eighteen to twenty-four year olds nearly doubled. A 1991 study published by the American Medical Association, however, caused public concern when it revealed that the character appealed to young children, who identified Old Joe as readily as Micky Mouse.*

ted, "I'm afraid of AIDS, so I'm sniffing."[28] Researchers predict that during the 1990s, more addicts will inhale or smoke heroin, rather than inject it. More potent blends of Asian heroin offset the decreased impact that inhaling and smoking the drug offers compared to injecting the sub-

A man who
shoots up can be
very giving.

He can give
you and your
baby AIDS.

Most babies with AIDS are born to mothers
who shot drugs or who sleep with men
who have.
Babies with AIDS are born to die.
If you're thinking of having a baby you and
your partner need to get tested for AIDS. Only

get pregnant when you're sure both of you
aren't infected. Until then help protect yourself
and your partner by using condoms.
And if your man shoots drugs, help him get
into treatment now. It could save three lives,
his, yours and your baby's.

STOP SHOOTING UP AIDS.
GET INTO DRUG TREATMENT
CALL 1-800 662 HELP.

He can give
you and your
baby AIDS.

get pregnant when you're sure both of you
aren't infected. Until then help protect yourself
and your partner by using condoms.
And if your man shoots drugs, help him get
into treatment now. It could save three lives,
ly   his, yours and your baby's.

OTING UP AIDS.
RUG TREATMENT
O 662 HELP.

He can give
you and your
baby AIDS.

get pregnant when you're sure both of you
aren't infected. Until then help protect yourself
and your partner by using condoms.
And if your man shoots drugs, help him get
into treatment now. It could save three lives,
is, yours and your baby's.

G UP AIDS.
AYMENT
2 HELP.

■ *Whether addressed to whites, blacks, or Hispanics, the message of
these posters is the same—sex partners and children of IV drug users
are at high risk for contracting AIDS, Acquired Immune Deficiency
Syndrome. AIDS does not discriminate among age, sex, race, or religion. Nevertheless, the infection rate for minority women, in particular, has steadily risen. The incidence of AIDS among black women is
more than twelve times higher than for white women; Hispanic
women face a rate eight times higher than whites.*

stance. Mindful of a likely rise in heroin demand,
South American drug dealers have greatly increased
poppy cultivation. During one raid in the summer
of 1991, Colombian police discovered an operation
that alone encompassed three thousand acres of
opium poppies. A frustrated Colombian official
explains, "The problem here is much greater than
poppies. My people grow poppies because of the
terrible level of poverty here. We need a develop-

ment plan from the states, not seizure of our crops."[29] As production of the drug rises, the twentieth century may well come full circle, closing as it began, with a declining use of drugs among the middle class and an escalating use of heroin among the poor. And so the cycle goes.

NOTES

1. David Pichaske, *A Generation in Motion*, (New York: Schirmer Books, 1979), 117.

2. H. Wayne Morgan, *Drugs in America: A Social History, 1800–1980,* (Syracuse: Syracuse University Press, 1981), 154.

3. Bill Hanson, ed., *Life with Heroin,* (Lexington, Mass.: Lexington Books, 1985), 83.

4. "Ecstasy," *Life,* August 1985, 90.

5. David Musto, *The American Disease Origins of Narcotic Control,* (New York: Oxford University Press, 1987), 254.

6. Edward Brecher, *Licit and Illicit Drugs,* (Boston: Little, Brown and Company, 1972), 292.

7. Peter Bogdanovich, *The Killing of the Unicorn: Dorothy Stratten 1960–1980* (New York: Bantam Books, 1985), 143.

8. Brecher, *Licit,* 248.

9. David Courtwright, *Addicts Who Survived,* (Knoxville: The University of Tennessee Press, 1989), 74–75.

10. Erich Goode, *Drugs in American Society,* (New York: McGraw Hill, 1989), 225.

11. Courtwright, *Addicts,* 320, 325.

12. A. Less Fritschler, *Smoking and Politics,* (Englewood Cliffs, N.J.: Prentice Hall, 1975), 2.

13. Musto, *Disease,* 254.

14. Courtwright, *Addicts,* 351.

15. Musto, *Disease,* 257.

16. Ibid., 264.

17. Ibid., 265.

18. Bender, David L. and Bruce Leonoe. *Drug Abuse: Opposing Viewpoints,* (San Diego: Greenhaven Press, 1988), 22.

19. M. Kathleen Wagner, "Drug Tests Becoming More Common in the Workplace," *Democrat and Chronicle* (Rochester, N.Y., 22 February 1992), 3.

20. John Hanchette, "Is the U.S. War on Drugs Working?" *Democrat and Chronicle*, (Rochester, N.Y., 2 July 1990), 5A.

21. Goode, *Drugs,* 269.

22. John Marshall, "Hidden Agendas in the War on Drugs," *Magazine of History* (Vol. 6, No. 2, Fall 1991), 30.

23. Milton Friedman, "A War We're Losing," *Wall Street Journal,* (7 March 1991), 314A.

24. Keith Schneider, "Drunk Driving," *The New York Times* (30 January 1991).

25. George Hacker, Ronald Collins, and Michael Jacobson, *Marketing Booze to Blacks* (Washington D.C.: Center for Science in the Public Interest, 1987), vii–viii.

26. *The Economist*, (London, Vol. 323, No. 7759, 16 May 1992), 24.

27. Goode, *Drugs*, 255.

28. Joseph B. Treaster, "To Avoid AIDS, Users of Heroin Shift from Injecting to Inhaling," *The New York Times*, (17 November 1991).

29. "Colombian Heroin May Be Increasing," *The New York Times* (27 October 1991), 15A.

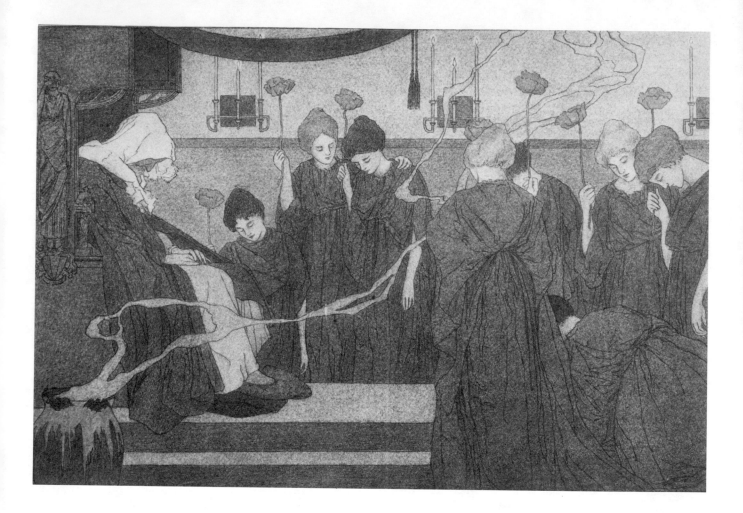

EPILOGUE

Drug use and anxiety about drug use has sounded a recurrent theme throughout America's history, from its earliest days to its most recent. For better or for worse, the desire to alter one's state of consciousness is part of the human condition whether it involves escape from boredom or pain, a curious journey into the unknown, or the pursuit of pleasure. While Americans have always had the tendency to use drugs, mainstream America's tendency to tolerate drug use has fluctuated.

Society remains ambivalent about drug use until it perceives either a real or imaginary threat. In the 1820s, that threat was the sharply rising number of drunkards who were unable to function within an increasingly industrial society. As more and more drunkards and their families filled hospitals, prisons, and poorhouses, the nation responded with a temperance movement that did in fact reduce the drinking rate.

Likewise, between the 1960s and 1980s the number of Americans killed in automobile accidents involving alcohol escalated until it reached unacceptable levels and prompted a national public outcry. At the same time, casualties mounted from cocaine and heroin use. In addition to the human losses came the conviction that illicit drugs were destroying the inner cities, spiking the crime rate, spreading the dreaded disease AIDS and sabotaging the productivity of factories and businesses.

Mainstream America entered a new age of temperance in the 1980s in reaction to the woes caused directly by illicit drug use and by fears of national decline. As historian David Musto observes, the modern temperance movement is further linked to the broader concerns about the environment and the quest for healthier, more natural, chemical-free living. As in the past, many Americans have responded to the complexities of drug use with simplistic approaches: just say no, declare war on drugs, increase the DEA's budget, get rid of the dealer and the user. None of these solutions have proved terribly successful. In fact, the efforts to incarcerate drug users have overwhelmed the prison and court systems, enmeshing the incarcerated user further in the criminal subculture. As author Erich Goode writes, "The fact is, in the United States, the recreational use of drugs is probably an intractable problem. . . . It is important to pursue policies that will be, if not good, then at least not disastrous." A striking example of a disastrous policy is the DEA's censure of clean needle exchange programs aimed at curbing HIV infection rates. As indicated by the program instituted in New Haven, Connecticut, and Vancouver, British Columbia, such public services reduces the spread of AIDS among IV drug users and the general population.

As Americans debate the many issues surrounding illicit drug use, such as the legality of drug testing, ironies emerge regarding the use of licit drugs. Tobacco, a product subsidized by the federal government and supported by powerful tobacco lobbies, claims in excess of 400,000 American lives annually. Another 100,000 Americans die from alcohol-related illnesses, accidents, homicides, and suicides. Cocaine and heroin use, by contrast, killed 4,678 in 1989. As pharmacologist Edgar Adams, Jr. notes, if either tobacco or alcohol were introduced today as a new consumer product, neither one would receive FDA approval.

Where does this complexity and contradiction lead? One approach might involve a reevaluation of recreational drugs, both licit and illicit, their health risks, and the setting of realistic goals aimed at reducing the harm that the most dangerous of these drugs cause their users and society. Such an approach could possibly involve the decriminalization of marijuana and the gradual withdrawal of tobacco subsidies. Certainly any approach to the drug problem should include more aggressive and widespread educational programs aimed at both adult and student populations. It is naive to seek complete eradication of illicit recreational drug use, but it may be possible to contain the damage it causes, altering—if not completely breaking—the cyclical pattern of drug use that has so troubled America's past.

SUGGESTED READINGS

Bender, David L., and Bruno Leonoe. *Drug Abuse: Opposing Viewpoints*. San Diego:
    Greenhaven Press, 1988.

Bernards, Neal, ed. *War on Drugs: Opposing Viewpoints*. San Diego: Greenhaven
    Press, 1990.

Blocker, Jack S., Jr., ed. *Alcohol, Reform and Society: The Liquor Issue in Social
    Context*. Contributions in American History, No. 83. Westport, Conn.:
    Greenwood Press, 1979.

_____. *"Give to the Winds Thy Fears": The Women's Temperance Crusade,
    1873–1874*. Contributions in Women's Studies, No. 55. Westport, Conn.:
    Greenwood Press, 1985.

Bordin, Ruth. *Frances Willard: A Biography*. Chapel Hill: University of North
    Carolina Press, 1986.

_____. *Woman and Temperance: The Quest for Power and Liberty,
    1873–1900*. Philadelphia: Temple University Press, 1981.

Boyer, Paul. *Urban Masses and Moral Order in America, 1820–1920*. Cambridge:
    Harvard University Press, 1978.

Brecher, Edward M. *Licit and Illicit Drugs*. Boston: Little, Brown and Company,
    1972.

Byck, Robert. *Cocaine Papers by Sigmund Freud*. New York: Stonehill, 1974.

Courtwright, David, Herman Joseph, and Don Des Jarlais. *Addicts Who Survived*.
    Knoxville: The University of Tennessee Press, 1989.

Duis, Perry R. *The Saloon: Public Drinking in Chicago and Boston, 1880–1920*. Urbana and Chicago: University of Illinois Press, 1983.

Furnas, Joseph. *The Life and Times of the Late Demon Rum*. New York: G. P. Putnam's Sons, 1965.

Goode, Erich. *Drugs in American Society*. New York: McGraw-Hill, Inc. 1989.

Helmer, John. *Drugs and Minority Oppression*. New York: Seabury Press, 1975.

Hooker, Richard. *Food and Drink in America*. New York: The Bobbs-Merrill Company, Inc., 1981.

Jaffe, Jerome, Robert Petersen, and R. Hodgson. *Addictions: Issues and Answers*. New York: Harper and Row, 1980.

Julien, Robert M., M.D. *A Primer of Drug Action*. 5th ed. New York: W. H. Freeman, 1988.

Kerr, K. Austin. *Organized for Prohibition: A New History of the Anti-Saloon League*. New Haven: Yale University Press, 1985.

Lender, Mark, and James Kirby Martin. *Drinking in America*. New York: Free Press, 1982.

McWilliams, John C. *The Protectors: Harry J. Anslinger and the Federal Bureau of Narcotics, 1930–1962*. Newark, Del.: University of Delaware, 1990.

Milkman, Harvey, and Stanley Sunderwirth. *Craving for Ecstasy: The Consciousness and Chemistry of Escape*. Lexington, Mass.: D.C. Heath and Company, 1987.

Morgan, H. Wayne. *Drugs in America: A Social History, 1800–1980*. Syracuse, N.Y.: Syracuse University Press, 1981.

Musto, David F. *The American Disease*. New Haven: Yale University Press, 1973.

Palmer, Cynthia, and Micheal Horowitz. *Shaman Woman, Mainline Lady*. New York: Quill, 1982.

Pichaske, David. *A Generation in Motion*. New York: Schirmer Books, 1979.

Pinney, Thomas. *A History of Wine in America from the Beginnings to Prohibition*. Berkeley: University of California Press, 1989.

Rorabaugh, W. J. *The Alcoholic Republic*. New York and Oxford: Oxford University Press, 1979.

Siegel, Ronald K. *Intoxication: Life in Pursuit of Artificial Paradise*. New York: E. P. Dutton, 1989.

Snyder, Solomon H. *Brainstorming: The Science and Politics of Opiate Research*. Cambridge: Harvard University Press, 1989.